Writing the Broadway Musical

Aaron Frankel

DRAMA BOOK PUBLISHERS

New York

Drama Book Publishers,
P.O. Box 816, Gracie Station   New York, NY 10028
Library of Congress Cataloging in Publication Data

Frankel, Aaron.
  Writing the Broadway musical.

  1. Music, Popular (Songs, etc.)—Writing and publishing.   2. Musical revue, comedy, etc.—Instruction and
study.   3. Playwriting.   I. Title.
MT67.F78   782.8'1'028   76-58925

Printed in the United States of America

ISBN 0-89676-044-8

To My Wife
Hail to thee, blithe Spirit!

Acknowledgments

This book, based on my working experience as a director and writer-collaborator in musical theater, arose from a workshop course I teach at The New School for Social Research in New York City. My students helped me refine my thoughts consistently and significantly. Dean Allen Austill and his staff provided important encouragement and support.

I owe special thanks to my New School teaching and professional colleague, composer Kenneth Jacobson, for acute and generous contributions. Certain aspects were reinforced by the "Round Tables" on musical theater held over the past years by the Workshop Foundation of my professional union, the Society of Stage Directors and Choreographers. Led by eminent directors and choreographers, these were craft discussions of the challenges, troubles and pleasures of creating musical theater, Broadway and Off Broadway.

I pay crowning tribute to what I have learned from writers and actors, and especially audiences.

Linda Readerman's editorial concerns for style and organization, and Melanie Ray's copyediting cares, also contributed to my education and enjoyment in writing this book. Most instrumental of all was the rigorous and inspiring counsel proferred by a most devoted friend, Abetha Aayer.

It is impossible to thank my wife, but I clearly know this book is as much hers as mine.

Contents

Introduction

Creating a musical can be one of the most satisfying experiences in theater. Part of its satisfaction is in conquering its mountainous odds. From its opening steps to the New York opening night, the work never stops. That a show is not written but rewritten applies above all to a musical. That a show is not written but wrought applies even more.

The difficulties start with understanding the differences between musicals and straight plays, and then the differences among musicals. Since the former will be a primary subject throughout this book, a guide to the latter would be a good place to begin.

Musicals may loosely be classified into six main "types," and form a spectrum:

Revue	/	Musical Comedy	/	Musical Drama	/	"Broadway Opera"	/	"New" Operetta	/	Play-with-Music

All spectrum bands fade into each other. Defining the two types at each end first, however, will make clear why the four middle ones comprise the heart of musical theater.

The revue is a series of separate songs, dances and skits, unified by a point of view, usually comic, and a distinct style of presenta-

1

tion. However, it is not unified by a through-story with developing characters—or *book*—and book musicals are musical theater's core. Among themselves, revues vary their styles widely, and strike different balances of comedy, song and dance each time. Any two random choices, from **New Faces** to **Oh, Calcutta!**, show the contrast.

The play-with-music is what many laypersons confuse with a musical. In this form, however, the plot can stand by itself without the music. The songs will illustrate or comment, and they will certainly increase the enjoyment. But the plot will remain intact without them, the songs are not pivotal. There is no *book* in the sense of plot and dialogue propelled by music and dance leading the action. **Marat/Sade** is a pure example of such a play-with-music, but a more apt illustration is **1776.** One song in it, "Molasses to Rum," makes **1776** a musical in particular instead of the play-with-music it is in general—because taking out the song leaves a hole. The plot cannot resume without picking up where the action of *the song* left off.

Of the four central musical theater types, musical comedy is still the most prevalent. One of the sources of musical comedy was the revue. The revue's bits and pieces began to be tied together by a book, resulting in early musical comedy hits like **No, No, Nanette** or **DuBarry Was a Lady** which had loosely constructed plots with the free-wheeling pliancy of revues, interrupting as they pleased for comedy turns or vehicle numbers by stars or specialty performers. Comedy still dominated, though plots were gradually treated more strictly, with better-motivated songs and better-related dances, until finally musical comedy reached the integrated heights of shows ranging from **Annie Get Your Gun** to **Guys and Dolls** to **Company.**

Musical comedy in turn gave rise to musical drama (also called the musical play). The short, joke rhythms of comedy gave way to longer-rhythmed dramatic emphases, and the music grew more ambitious. It first appeared in 1927, in **Show Boat,** the show which also pioneered the "integrated musical," in which score and plot support each other, and extraneous material is, for the most part, pared away. Drama continued to take over other musicals, character development grew more complex in both song and dialogue, subplots were better connected and comedy threw shadows or served only as relief. Resulting musicals ranged from **Pal Joey** to **Gypsy** to **Fiddler on the Roof** to **Raisin.** Other musical dramas took an opposite course, minimizing one element: dialogue. From **West Side Story** to **Ain't Supposed To Die a Natural Death**, song and dance carried the story far more than spoken words. Only recently has this innovative approach begun to receive the development due it.

"Broadway opera" (to coin a term) was the next step up from musical drama. Neither traditional nor modern opera is musical theater, strictly speaking, because they tend to be static rather than move, much less dance, and because they employ music from classical sources and as the dominating element. "Broadway opera" also emphasizes music to a greater degree than any of the other musical theater types, but the music originates out of popular sources and is held in balance with all the other elements in the musical. Both opera and "Broadway opera" lean to the spectacular, but in content and treatment, "Broadway opera" is vernacular, not literary. It has ranged from **Porgy and Bess** to **The Most Happy Fella** to **Jesus Christ Superstar.** It is the area most heralded for future development.

Related to "Broadway opera" are new versions of the old operetta form. Old operetta includes the romantic musicals of Victor Herbert (**Naughty Marietta**), Rudolf Friml (**Rose-Marie**) and Sigmund Romberg (**The Desert Song**), written under the European influence of Offenbach, Lehar, Oskar Straus and Johann Strauss II. The last "old operetta" on Broadway was **The Song of Norway** in 1944. The new versions are more characteristically American, if not in subject, then in treatment. They are exemplified by the musicals **Carousel, The King and I** and others by Rodgers and Hammerstein, and such additional ones as far apart in style as **Kismet** and **The Fantasticks. Brigadoon** has turned into an operetta for current audiences. "New" operetta is still lyrical above all and still emphasizes fantasy, but now reflects the real world rather than escapes it, unlike old operetta.

These "types" are merely compass points to steer by in creating musicals. Observed rigidly, they are confining; many musicals overlap these classifications. Is **My Fair Lady**, for instance, musical comedy, musical drama or new operetta? Which type is the highly innovative **A Little Night Music?** Is **Hair** a rock operetta, or a barely concealed revue? Is **Grease** a throwback to revue, or a new form of it? Most of its songs arise suddenly and are indirectly motivated, but are joined so playfully together that episodes become a book. In the revised seventies' book and production of **Candide**, the songs are better motivated than in the original. Yet is not the show a modern, glorified form of revue?

At the opposite end, is **Lady in the Dark** a play-with-music, or is it a musical drama? With its preponderance of straight dialogue, it seems solely a play-with-music. Yet all its songs arrive with such force, in the form of Liza's dreams, that they take over not only the stage but the plot, in the manner of full musical drama. Where, finally, does **A Chorus Line** fit? It revitalizes the neglected trend of the "ballet musical" represented by **West Side Story**, joins comedy and drama, and once more newly mints revue into book. But its unique enfolding of monologue/dialogue within song within dance makes it a fresh development of its own.

These are but a few examples of the American musical's bottomless vitality. It keeps finding new ways of using song, dance and dialogue, and new combinations of them.

When Jerry Bock, composer of **Fiddler on the Roof**, was asked which comes first, the music or the words, he replied, "The book, of course." It is the procedure to follow.

The Basic Elements of a Musical

Seed
Story
Spirit
Sound and Look
Point of View
Sum: Style

A *lead sheet* specifies everything that is basic to a song. The book may be regarded as the lead sheet of a musical. It contains everything that appears on the stage. Songwriters who expect to write the songs by themselves and leave the bookwriting to someone else are picking the hardest way to get the songs right.

This is difficult for beginners to recognize. All the collaborators must work out the book together because song and dance are as fundamental to it as the dialogue, and count even more. Indeed, two otherwise dissimilar seventies musicals, **Ain't Supposed To Die a Natural Death** and **Jesus Christ Superstar**, proceed in a flow of songs without a single word of dialogue, yet both have plots, though episodic and "non-linear," which tell complete and complex stories. Both abound with book.

"Book trouble" only means that the elements not put to music fail in craft or in imagination to match those which are. The drop from one energy level to the other shows through.

5

Seed

What the musical starts from personally is the key to the entire project. *Personal* means not merely what interests but what spurs a writer to write the show. It may come from anywhere: an impulse or an inspiration, sudden protest or old ambition, a passing word or a profound involvement, a glimpse of a story or only a flash of music or lyric. Any *seed* that becomes a passion means a start, and if it stays a passion, a finish.

The seed is what all the upcoming struggle revolves around. It is most in jeopardy of being dislodged or crushed by the tremendous buffetings of the writing and production processes. The collaborator who throughout can preserve the seed saves everyone agony, and may even save the show. The seed may alter, but only to become clearer, not different. It cannot, of course, be the same for every collaborator, but all the collaborators must be able to graft themselves to it.

The seed of a musical also has an objective derivation. What generically makes a musical? Either its idea fits musical theater innately, or must be translated into it. There are three essentials: does it eliminate the "fourth wall?" does it sing? does it dance?; and one more essential: does it do all three?

There are two ways of making theater: behind the "fourth wall," or through the "fourth wall." A *picture stage* frames the story in three walls, rear and sides; they are visible. In front is the "fourth wall," invisible but most present of all, because the actors create it. They behave as if they are living behind it; their energy runs among them, while the audience "eavesdrops" on them through the make-believe wall. On a *platform stage*, the stage energy drives out to address the audience directly. No "fourth wall" stands between the audience and the actors. Instead of using the stage as a picture frame within which to *represent* a "real life" event, it is used as a springboard upon which to *present* a theater event. Musicals are prime examples of platform theater; this may be partly why we invariably call a musical a show and not a play.

While it is true that in practice picture theater and platform theater are never pure but overlap, one always governs. One-hundred-year-old picture theater covers all the naturalistic or realistic plays. Three-thousand-year-old platform theater includes all Oriental theater, all dance theater, Greek and Elizabethan theater, concerts and vaudeville, and epic and absurdist theater as well as environmental and street theater.

Some people claim that the musical is improving because it is becoming more realistic. This is to misconstrue what platform theater does in general, and how a musical differs from a straight play in particular. Musical theater may be getting more real, but not more realistic. A realistic play closes in on its subject, while a musical book opens up its subject, freeing it to become less literal.

The straight play **My Sister Eileen**, for instance, takes place in a one-set interior, "a one-room basement studio near Christopher Street" in Greenwich Village. Its musical adaptation, **Wonderful Town**, takes place in eight locations over thirteen scenes, moving from the studio, now used only twice, into Christopher Street four times, the studio's brick backyard twice, a Village nightclub once and the street in front of it once; and goes outside the Village also, once to a police station, to a mid-town publishing office, and all the way to the Brooklyn Navy Yard for its Act I climax—the famous conga scene. As a result, the musical enlarged its subject, the New York merry-go-round. Much like the hit of the seventies, **Raisin**, musicals have often given more point and texture to their stories than the originals from which they were taken.

The difference is the fourth wall. Retained, it encloses and intensifies, which serves the gradual, microscopic method of realism. Removed, it releases and expands, which serves the swift, telescopic method of musicals.

Music lends wings to this release. Here is the second essential, that songs take over most of the main points of the plot, and make them the high points. Other unique musical devices—*establishing numbers, reprises, segues, underscoring*—will further integrate all the elements. Since conflict makes drama, it will be show music that will raise its pressures or discharge them. Musical theater suits the action to the music, and the music to the action.

In **My Fair Lady**, for example, "The Rain in Spain" is a major turning-point in the plot. As Colonel Pickering watches another speech lesson, Professor Higgins and Eliza grow increasingly more tense. "The rain in Spain lies mainly in the plain" is repeated, over and over. The words begin the lightest beat; the music under is barely perceptible. Suddenly, astonishingly, Eliza gets it! The moment explodes into song, dance and a triumphant celebration. It works all the more because Lerner and Loewe (suiting music to the action) choose a tango rhythm—cool British reserve bursts into torrid Latin passion.

Its yield, unforeseen, was enormous. It not only did away with pages of dialogue, as planned, but also dispensed with a ballet, two songs and some scenery. The ballet originally seemed necessary to summarize Eliza's progress in dress, manners and deportment. Two songs would then follow the ballet: Higgins's "Come to the Ball" to Eliza, and her answer, "Say a Prayer for Me Tonight." "The Rain in Spain" worked so completely, however, that all three numbers were cut very early in the out-of-town tryout period. (Eliza's song was salvaged for **Gigi**.)

It is very hard for playwrights, especially those with a realistic bent, to accept that songs heighten action more than dialogue, and in addition, take over most of the climaxes. Songs can cover more ground more quickly. Here is something fundamental: a song that works in a musical *compresses and expands* at the same time. The book for a musical needs actions high enough to break into songs.

The third essential is that this musical energy also break out into physical energy. Dance is physical music. The quantity of dance in musicals may vary widely, but even in those with little—**South Pacific, The Fantasticks, A Funny Thing Happened on the Way To The Forum, Mame** or **Zorba**—the *spirit* of dance animates them. This spirit got **My Fair Lady** out of the chairs of **Pygmalion** *to stay* on its feet; small wonder that following the celebration of "The Rain in Spain," Eliza sings, "I Could Have *Danced* All Night." In reverse, **Guys and Dolls** moves so vigorously that near the end it needs to brace itself, with "*Sit Down*, You're Rockin' the Boat." "Country" waltz imbues **Carousel**, European waltz buoys **A Little Night Music** and each spins its world like a motor. All musicals move: next to the circus, musicals are the most physical kind of theater.

There are many kinds of dance spirit, and the individuality of many musicals is defined by them. Upbeat like **My Fair Lady** and **Guys and Dolls**, downbeat like **Carousel** or **West Side Story**, or offbeat like **A Little Night Music** or **Grease, Company** or **Pal Joey**, the biggest effect of every good musical is its lift. This lift is the physical release and joy of dance, our American second nature.

Story

The first issue of the seed is the *story*. It essentializes all the seeding and shapes all the growing. Up to this point the seed ideas have been intuited. Now they must be executed—the work of craft.

Story is fundamental and does not mean *plot*. **Romeo and Juliet** and **West Side Story** tell the same story, but their plots are very different. The story is what holds the plot together—its through line; the plot is the working out of the story, its developments in detail. Stories may be summed up—as in headlines or newspaper leads, or blurbs for books, films or TV shows. Plots have component parts—situations, time and place, actions, characters, dialogue, and in musical theater, song and dance. It is true that good stories may say more than one thing. But they "turn" on only one thing, one main event or drive. Will Oedipus root out the murderer? Will Hamlet avenge his father? Will Jack and Algernon be Ernest?

A common way of starting is to outline a plot. But this is the hardest way, full of struggles, because there is no story foundation to build on. When there is a foundation, not one but many plots suggest themselves. The longer plotting is delayed, in fact, the sooner collaborators may see the *story* on which to concur. Often the collaborators keep telling different stories, but do not find it out until exhausted by plot-devising. Condense the story first into a simple, complete sentence—subject, verb, object. Above all, begin with a conflict between *persons,* not ideas. Who does what to whom?

My Fair Lady and **Company**, a classic musical and an innovative contemporary one, will provide the backbone of examples throughout this book. To begin. The story of **My Fair Lady** is: a man transforms a girl, and *vice versa.* That the girl also transforms the man, the vice versa, is the important story difference from **Pygmalion**, the musical's touch, making it a love story. The story of **Company**, an adaptation from seven original one-act playlets, is: bachelor holds off friends. "Bachelor" is the exact subject; "a man" would be too general here. "Friends," though a plural, general object, is still personal.

Looser story statements—such as that **My Fair Lady** is about the clash of the British classes, or that **Company** is about the difficulties of commitment—should be avoided. They are not active and concrete enough to supply controls. The biggest control of all is the verb. "Transform" and "hold off," for instance, not only define the main action of each story, but even catch something of the spirit. Above all, concrete verbs help to exclude "meanings" from the story line. What matters is not what the story is about but *what makes it happen.* Characters in action, which is the only way an audience will take sides, is the only way an audience will care about meanings. That is why the best stories are usually fables as well, because the morals are inherent.

The exact story may take time to find. It took almost all the out-of-town tryout period, for instance, for the story of **Company** to jell. Not until its climax song, "Being Alive," emerged from three previous song efforts did the story of Robert resolve itself. But the germ of it, some direction for Robert's life to take, existed from the beginning. No matter the final changes, a story without a starting definition is hopeless—plotting and re-plotting take over and never end. Condensed, concrete *story* is all the outline needed.

Defining the story of **Company** for these pages illustrates some other pitfalls in the process. Although I finally chose "holds off," this is still too negative and passive a verb to play; something more active is needed, and so I am substituting "tests out." The plural object "friends" poses another danger—it may remain general when the need is to develop specific core relationships from it. In **Company**, no such dramatic focus took over. Adding confusion was the reappearing red flag of marriage: it was only the context or *situation*, an important plot component but not the story handle. Consequently, the chief problem in this trail-blazing show of so many virtues is that bachelor Robert remained merely an observing character, a device to connect the original playlets but not bringing any central conflicts up front. Stakes for the audience were not high enough.

The suggestions of the **My Fair Lady** and **Company** story lines are not the only possibilities, but any definitions now are hindsight, and hindsight is beside the point. The function of *story* is to bring forethought to the process of creating the musical and to provide basic agreement for collaborators to work from.

Once there is a story, a particular way of telling it in musical theater follows. The story must thrust through the fourth wall, enjoy the wide-wheeling freedoms of the platform stage. The story must be *opened up*. Straight plays physically close in their stories by sticking to the most concentrated and fewest locations. The book of a musical physically opens up its story by rapid shifting among the most dynamic, diverse locations. A play inhabits places; a musical goes places.

The most famous example of "opening up" is **My Fair Lady**. Earlier efforts to adapt **Pygmalion** into a musical had defeated several writers, including Rodgers and Hammerstein. It almost defeated Lerner and Loewe as well, until they came upon the idea of bringing the play's offstage events on stage. Now the most celebrated though not the first instance of the use of such a solution, it unlocked all the previous difficulties, and led, including reprises, to two-thirds of the songs and places finally employed. The significant fact is that all these songs and scenes are either *public moments* or happen in *public places*, or both. Expanding the world of the story means making the largest use of the stage. This is how to open up.

It does not mean adding people or noise, but theatrical places and dimensions. **I Do! I Do!** illustrates an extreme example of the problem of opening up. Its source, a straight play, **The Fourposter**, seems severely limited for adaptation into a musical. It has only one location, a bedroom, and a cast of only two. The remedy was to make the defects into virtues. The single setting was maintained, but it was opened up by projecting through the bedroom walls— especially the fourth. The stage was extended by a runway, around the orchestra pit and into the audience. The two characters could move out onto the limbo of the runway and use it for the special places of their world: free suggestions of weddings and holidays, arrivals and departures, the vaudeville scenes of life. In tandem, the physical scene-shifts in the bedroom, denoting changes in the family fortunes, danced on and off too. Bedrooms are for dreaming.

The original straight play consisted of the main events in a marriage, from the wedding night to old age; in the musical, the progression became a parade. The cast of two characters was not increased, but they were enlarged. Abetted by superstar casting (Mary Martin and Robert Preston), they became high-powered vehicle roles, representing a middle-class everyman and everywoman. The song and dance that husband and wife now literally gave each other made the musical once again broader and more pertinent than the original play.

My Fair Lady and **I Do! I Do!** are accomplished facts. How does one open up material yet to be made into a musical? An exercise to open up any existing story (from my New School workshop, "Writing for the Musical Theater,") will illustrate. In this case, two plays were proposed.

In its original form, **The Male Animal** takes place in "the living room of the house of Professor Tommy Turner, in a mid-western university town." Here, the means to open it up physically was not the place but the time. The story happens over a big-game football weekend. The first scene, thus, might be a tailgate picnic in the stadium parking lot, where friends could stop off—using an American tribal-love ritual motif long before **Hair**. Indeed, all the main characters and situations could be introduced, at one time in one place. Parts of crowds, football teams or marching bands could also pass by, or could be heard and "seen" offstage. In short, songs and production numbers could take over freely and with zest, and the book could be populated immediately. What took far more time to present in the original could now center, in a rapid and concentrated start, on all the main relationships, with the content, rhythm and style of the musical established at the curtain's rise. The next scene could go anywhere.

All of **Born Yesterday** also takes place in only one setting—a duplex suite of the best hotel in Washington, D.C. The suite is "a masterpiece of offensive good taste," at the then going rate (right after World War II) of "two hundred and thirty-five dollars a day." Here was a built-in musical comedy springboard of a scene, demanding a switch neither of time nor place, only building upon. Thus, the red carpet arrival of the "just not couth," wheeling-dealing junk tycoon, Harry Brock, trailed by his "dumb broad," Billie Dawn, would progress in flourishes. The entourage sent by the hotel to receive them would grow from maids, valets, barber, manicurist, masseurs and bellhops to assistant managers and private secretaries. The entourage arriving in other step-ups would involve personal maids and valets, bodyguards, lawyers, press agents, Representatives, Senators, more secretaries. Crisscross "Rockette" routines, fanfares, alarms and excursions, and at last enter Harry, enter Billie, in full regalia. There may be other ways or different details, but the moment is a musical comedy entrance if ever there was one. Again, the next scene could go anywhere.

Building up such natural high-voltage situations in a musical means adding details that essentialize, not that are merely documentary. The expansion works only if it produces a compression of the situation at the same time, the **Born Yesterday** example, or if the compression produces an expansion, **The Male Animal** example—the same principle that makes a song in a musical work. Opening up is likewise a process of heightening.

As already noted, **Wonderful Town** expanded its place from one setting to several in surrounding Greenwich Village, and then to New York City beyond that. **I Do! I Do!** covered a fifty-year marriage by pushing out bedroom walls as far as they could go. The specific places added by **My Fair Lady** were:

> street outside Higgins's house, three times
> outside Doolittle's tenement-section pub, two times
> Ascot race track
> Ascot tent
> Embassy Promenade
> Embassy Ballroom
> Covent Garden Flower Market
> upstairs hall in Higgins's house
> conservatory (changed from drawing room) at Higgins's
> mother's house

All three musicals reached for the liveliest physical places most apt to open up the stories they had to tell. So must all musicals.

Having gotten **The Male Animal** and **Born Yesterday** started as musicals, to keep them opened up would be the next problem. What lively additional places could they go? It is coincidental, by the way, that the hypothetical scenes described above happen to be opening scenes; openings, however, are a problem of their own. *Opening up* is the *sole* subject here.

Places that continue to open up **The Male Animal** might be:

> porch and front lawn of house
> backyard of house
> upstairs bedroom or hallway
> local drinking and eating hangouts ("Hennick's")
> campus dining room
> campus training table
> football locker room
> fraternity row
> fraternity house lounge
> dorm lounge
> campus lit magazine office
> campus gym dance
> faculty conference room
> trustees' board room
> Dean's office and hallway outside
> "Keller Building" lobby
> Keller's colossal office . . . etc. . . . .

Places that continue to open up **Born Yesterday** may be even easier to conjure, because of the Washington, D.C. locale:

> hotel areas: lobby, corridors, elevators, bar, dining rooms, meeting rooms, other suites (the lawyer's) and hotel rooms (the reporter's)
> parks and park benches
> outside the White House grounds
> the Supreme Court chamber
> galleries of Congress
> cloak rooms and caucus rooms
> a display in the National Gallery
> a display in the Smithsonian
> Capitol steps
> Lincoln and Jefferson Memorials
> top of the Washington Monument

Congressman's garden party
a concert hall
a theater lobby
Brentano's book store . . . etc. . . .

Obviously, more places (including "crazy" ones) might be imagined for each list. Not all will prove usable, while some will prove usable more than once. Those usable at all, however, will meet two criteria. First, the very thought of them as places will inspire plot ideas which would never occur otherwise. The longer the list, the more plot ideas will evolve. The power of suggestion, working this way, is boundless; and the freedom from plotting constrictions is astonishing.

Second, the most workable places will provide the spring and space to sing and dance. A book opens up a musical's story by finding the turned-out, public places and moments of most urgency or spark, the naturals of music and dance. Theater is "three boards and a passion," the imagination's platform; it is Shakespeare's way, and the musical is nearest his method.

Spirit

The sheer energy of opening up the story also leads to *turning out* the story. This externalizing is the spirit of all musical theater, making it so outer-directed that it embraces an audience.

The two archetypal stances in musicals are the solo actor-singer, arms outstretched, clasping the audience, and the couple singing to the audience, clasping each other. To capture the audience in these embraces is a large part of a musical's success. The embraces may differ widely, from a wave of the hand to bear hugs, including embraces in reverse, from upraised fists to the finger (**Ain't Supposed To Die a Natural Death, Hair**). In any form, the energy that embraces an audience to the last row of the balcony is one of the most exhilarating experiences the theater offers—and it starts with the writer.

This turning-out process is reinforced by the action of music itself; it goes out front. In concert, the musicians face out, the singer stands downstage and faces out. In dance, the pattern goes downstage and faces out. Musicals inject this turned-out energy into every aspect of their performance. The gentler ones merely embrace more softly. Fostering these impulses to embrace the audience is the way. The spirit of all musicals thrusts them outwards.

The spirit of any particular musical is not a matter of an academic label but a specific creative challenge. To call it comic, light-hearted, satiric, melodramatic or tragic, or a combination of these, is only a beginning. The particular spirit is best caught in the couching of the story itself. Amplifications may then follow.

The spirit of **My Fair Lady**, following its story definition, might then come to its comic battle of the sexes. Further aspects occur:

> witty, high-toned, elegant
> satiric, sardonic
> rowdy, brash
> comic class-warfare: brittle, cheeky, earthy
> metamorphoses by reversals

The spirit of **Company**, following its story definition, might then come to its tart delights in the marriage chase. Furthering its aspects produces:

> hip and wise guy and scared
> groupish and lonely
> clinical and spontaneous
> cutting and rueful
> playing roles and playing games
> dependence and independence
> paradoxes
> a left-handed hymn to New York
> mixing comedy of manners and theater of the absurd

These are intimations by which the spirit may animate.

Calling next on the senses will translate abstractions into concreteness. Metaphors, neologisms—whatever hits the fancy, no pondering or editing. Seize. Now the means is by impulse and free association, the flash of intuition, the *play* of imagination.

My Fair Lady:

> champagne in glasses that "ping," cut and polished gems
> ball gowns, hound's tooth checks
> the washed and the unwashed
> baggy pants, flowered straw hats
> tongue in cheek, thumb to nose
> bludgeon and rapier
> tug of war (several tugs: sex, class, power)

Company:

> metallic-clean colors, in high contrasts
> a mosaic of changes
> cool and hot, chic and brassy
> open language and closed hearts
> capers, couplings, and misery loves—company

These did not spring forth so sorted out and arranged, of course, nor are they always strictly of the senses. Neither does it matter if any of them will literally appear as images or objects in the ultimate production. What is important is to summon the spirit, and give it texture.

Sound and Look

The next step is to embody the spirit. What is the *overall sound* of the show, and its *overall look*?

More than song and dance are involved here. A musical has an inner music and an inner movement that anticipate song and dance. It has an orchestration of all its elements to be divined, a rhythm to be sensed. There is an encompassing vision to bring to it. If the writers imagine, so will the audience.

The imagining can be helped by free-form filling in of the sound and the look. *Story* and *spirit* have already been essentialized, but the story always needs more personifying, and the spirit more physicalizing. *Sound and look* are the ways to accomplish both these ends. The model that follows may be used for creating a new musical as much or as little as seems useful, in this arrangement or other arrangements. Its aim is simply to carry through what is seminal to the immediate and the specific.

Story	Spirit
My Fair Lady: *Sound*	
several long wails (Higgins', Eliza's, Doolittle's, Freddy's, Pickering's, others') some grunts and whispers hymns and hosannas befitting a tale of several metamorphoses	the growls and squeals the roars and shrieks the chirps, baas, moos and purrs of the battles of the sexes and the classes

My Fair Lady: *Look*

the studio of a magician
an alchemist's laboratory
the encircling, fixed
    Victorian world as proving
    ground

the seesaw of large open
    exteriors with cramped
    fussy interiors .
large rhythms and small
    rhythms (and their mixture)

Company: *Sound*

an incessant exchange of
    privacies
    bondings
    discords
    breaks
    re-tyings
polyphonies of
    psalms
    exhortations
    protests
    alarms
    deflations
    huzzahs
of giving and not giving in

the shouts and whispers
the guffaws, giggles and
    chuckles .
the wails, sobs and sighs
the overtones and
    undercurrents
of married life
of single life
of the gatherings of the
    young, making-out, middle
    class
the cacophonies, jolts and
    silences of New York
the comic-sad, driven, "real-
    vs.-fantasy" interchanging
    solos, duets, trios and
    choruses of all

Company: *Look*

a carousel of changing rides
    which may only be a
    treadmill
elevators, up and down, up
    and down
a fixed situation (35th
    birthday surprise party),
    à la theater of the absurd,
    fragmented to whirl around
    itself

free-wheeling and
    compartmentalized
split images and ups and
    downs
chrome and splash colors
Danish modern and stuffed
    cushions
high-rise terraces and low-
    down nightclubs
duplexes and walk-ups and
    pads
bright and low lights
shadows

Obviously some of this suggests pegs for eventual music and
lyrics, dialogue and dance, staging and scenery, and plotting. But
the more the sound and look are caught in essence, the more estab-

lished and colorful the world of the musical, and the characters who enliven it.

Fundamental to all this is rhythm. A musical is a literal transcription of rhythms and counter-rhythms. Rapid scene changes will thus be characteristic of musicals. Some recent musicals, such as **Sweet Charity, Promises, Promises** or **Raisin**, have longer single scenes, but there is always multiple and therefore rapid change. These changes fall into three categories: shifts of locales, shifts between small and large groups within locales, and always, sharp shifts of modes.

The first is obvious. The physical decor keeps changing settings and colors, the costumes inject more colors and shapes, and lighting sets off each image with further and crowning changes. The second covers an equally broad range. It alternates from the solo singing and dancing actor to the duet, the small group and the large ensemble, dissolving and re-forming, and changes the stage space continuously. These are scenes within scenes. Thirdly, every one of these locale or grouping changes is a shift of mode, of the moment's quality; and when nothing physical changes, any single actor or set of actors can shift from one mode to another.

A musical, in short, is a set of varied rhythmic impulses or charges. High or low, the *rhythmic contrast* between these charges is what makes them effective. Building strong, free and frequent contrasts, within a scene, and from scene to scene, creates a higher and higher lift. Pace is change of pace—rhythmic contrasts. The rhythm of things may be what an artist most transmutes. In the musical theater, it is physical instantly.

The complement of rhythmic contrasts is *visual variety*. Musical theater moves figures through mere signals of place, on an open platform of space, and keeps the space free for changes; this makes all musicals spectacles. Some may be simple and straightforward, like **She Loves Me!, Promises, Promises** or **You're a Good Man, Charlie Brown,** and others may be sensational, like **Kismet, Camelot, Hair** or **Follies,** but most are a wide-ranging combination, like **Hello, Dolly!, Your Own Thing, Cabaret** or **Fiddler on the Roof.**

In picture theater, the set has an immediate function, to define the place. It then recedes into the background, as actors take over the foreground. In musical theater, the changing setting shares the foreground, not only in decor, costuming and lighting, but in the physical staging itself, capped by dance. The more variety offered to the eye and ear, paradoxically, the more the audience's attention is kept. Musical writers must visualize as much as they musicalize. The two methods fortify each other.

Further, the musical is one of the last preserves of glamour and the exotic. Even when the subject is familiar, the musical employs what is exotic or glamorous in it, such as:

"Backstage"—
     In politics: **Fiorello!, Call Me Madam**
     In business: **The Pajama Game, How To Succeed in Business Without Really Trying**
     In sports: **Damn Yankees**
     In theater: **Kiss Me, Kate, Gypsy**

The "mythic" in city life—
     The Greenwich Villages around the world: **Wonderful Town, The Threepenny Opera,** and rock musicals like **Your Own Thing, Salvation**
     The fast life: **Mame, Promises, Promises, Company**
     Ethnic enclaves: **Raisin, Flower Drum Song, Milk and Honey, West Side Story, The Most Happy Fella, Guys and Dolls, Porgy and Bess**

"Mythic" figures—
     Winners and losers: **Of Thee I Sing, I'd Rather Be Right, Funny Girl**
     Folk characters: **Fiddler on the Roof, Annie Get Your Gun, Li'l Abner, Paint Your Wagon**

In short, the musical's arena is the outrageous, the wondrous, the screwball—life at full rhythm—and more common than we think. As Martha Graham puts it, the creative problem is not to be larger than life but as large.

Visual variety may also provide rhythmic contrasts within a single scene and heighten it enormously. Near the end of Act I of **West Side Story**, there is a quintet reprise of a duet first sung by the two leads, Tony and Maria, "Tonight." Checkered by light into five separate playing areas (called "space staging"), two parts of the stage contained the street gangs, while in the three other areas were Anita, Tony and Maria. Alone and together, from area to area, in song, dance and gesture, "Tonight" became a polyphonic stage montage. It condensed time and place, and fused conflicting actions into one mounting action. In short, the song itself formed the stage image. This is a power unique to musical theater, an eminent application of compression producing enlargement. It further pulled together all that had gone before, and set the fuse for all that was to come.

Not just individual songs but whole musicals may sometimes turn "simultaneous staging," as this technique is also called, to special vantage. **Hair** put time together in different combinations all through a single physical setting, a theater. **Company** broke time into pieces, departing from and returning to a single place, a New York bachelor apartment, thereby fragmenting and recondensing the image of its leading character, Robert, as seen by his friends. Instead of the barely concealed revue I first called it, **Hair** might be better described as a "collage," while **Company** emerges as "cubist" (a case that will be made fully in a later chapter). **Company** was also the farthest that simultaneous action through musical stage montages had yet gone, until **Follies** and the rewritten revival of **Candide** went farther.

Show music is *sound and look* in one. It is the original theater dissolve, or quick cut, cross cut, split screen, multiple exposure and, above all, wide-angle screen or close-up.

Point of View

If getting each collaborator to tell the same story from the beginning is one difficulty, unifying the *point of view* is even harder. It may even be more basic. For example, whose story is to be told, Cinderella's or the Prince's (**Camelot**), Jack the Giant-Killer's, or the Giant's (**Gypsy**)? The longer it takes to recognize and agree on whose story to tell, the longer everything else takes. The bookwriter will be puzzled over why the song seems wrong, the composer over why the lyrics seem off the point, the lyricist over why the dialogue seems on a different tack, everybody over why the story will not jell.

The collaborators may not even be speaking the same language. Someone may be talking *concept*, for instance, thinking that is a point of view. *Point* is not point of view. Concept and point are far removed from an *angle of vision*, an outlook through a character's eyes, from which to view the material. Concepts and points are often the most difficult to convey to others. Since by definition they are abstractions, not tools, they usually come out differently in the end as well. They are more likely to be only approaches to shows ("Let's put Macbeth into Prohibition Chicago"), or generalized ideas ("The drug scene is a Black Mass"). Even these can be made concrete, however, by inserting a point of view. Through whose eyes *may the audience see*? (Through the three witches, transformed into three retired molls trying to get back into the business. Through a group leader, passing pills as if holding communion.) The point of view is transferred to characters acting on their points of view, which the audience momentarily adopts.

Point of view is always concrete, and relative. I am a Northerner, but let Errol Flynn play "Johnny Reb" and I am for the South. I am outside looking in, but if I get inside, I am against the outsider. Viewpoints may differ toward the same thing and differ toward different things. This is of course a secret of dramatizing. Characters serve to personify several points of view a writer sometimes holds. Or a character may come alive from a writer's taking his point of view. Leave viewpoints out, however, and a central means of control, and even of imagination, vanishes.

In **My Fair Lady**, the writers' attitude is *satiric-comic*, using sharp but affectionate ridicule. This attitude is transferred into the way all the characters see each other, and sometimes themselves, while the audience sees the contradictions and imbalances the characters cannot. This is the comic vantage point. The audience's sense of reality is different from the characters', who are serving their points of view, while the audience enjoys its own. As already noted, further, **My Fair Lady**'s viewpoint is wider than **Pygmalion**'s. This is because, first, more of Eliza's viewpoint is included, which gives her character more facets, and she in turn transforms Higgins. Second, in opening up the story to incorporate Doolittle's working-class hangouts as well as upper class Ascot, the comedy of manners in which the class conflict is expressed becomes both broader and higher comedy. The more the characters know where they are, the more the audience knows where it stands.

The point of view in **Company** is a different case. Instead of assuming an established viewpoint on the audience's part, **Company** jolted it. The attitude of its writers is *ironic-comic*, in contrast to **My Fair Lady**'s *satiric-comic*. The distinction is one of greater detachment on the part of **Company**'s writers, an alienation which is more dry and cool. Paradox may be **Company**'s manner, but ambivalence is its result. It is easier to be witty than decisive about dilemmas.

This appealed to only one part of **Company**'s audience. Most audiences prefer a musical whose story is more conclusive, and expect characters and an atmosphere less acid. What was progressive and trail-blazing about **Company** also made it controversial. Had it embodied its attitude in more of the points of view of its characters, and above all focally in its leading character, the audience as a whole might have embraced it more.

Are there ways to implant unexpected or unpleasant points of view so that an audience will adopt them? Some plays, like **King Lear, The Way of the World, The Misanthrope, Mourning Becomes Electra,** do so. There are musicals that do so, too, by some similar devices: **Hair, Cabaret** and **Sweet Charity** all possess a fierceness of integrity and follow through, even of jolting viewpoints, that sweep along an audience. **Pal Joey** and **The Threepenny Opera** buttress themselves with so many props of charm, humor and invention that the audience is carried away, relieved that there but for the grace of God goes it. Means other than writing may help, such as casting, direction, choreography, design and performance, but they are partial. The basic solution is to reveal all characters as fully as possible, sympathetic or not, by closer connection of the audience to their points of view. The more an audience can share the points of view of different characters, the more its own open up.

Sometimes a song bears the show's viewpoint. **Company**'s score has in fact more than one possibility, since so many of its songs "comment" on the action. Not that commenting is the criterion; indeed, most show *point-of-view songs* are direct actions, such as "The Carousel Waltz" in **Carousel**, "You've Got To Be Taught" in **South Pacific**, "Let Me Entertain You" in **Gypsy**, "Tradition" in **Fiddler on the Roof**, and so forth. There are title songs, such as "Guys and Dolls," "Camelot," "Hello, Dolly!," "Jesus Christ Superstar" and "Company" which would similarly fit. But I feel the overall point of view of **Company** is represented by "Sorry-Grateful." Even though the musical may lack a large part of the audience's engagement through particular character points of view, this song sung by three husband friends to Robert reflects the underlying viewpoint shared by all, the irony of joy.

> YOU'RE ALWAYS SORRY,
> YOU'RE ALWAYS GRATEFUL,
> YOU'RE ALWAYS WOND'RING WHAT MIGHT HAVE BEEN,
> THEN SHE WALKS IN.
> AND STILL YOU'RE SORRY,
> AND STILL YOU'RE GRATEFUL,
> AND STILL YOU WONDER AND STILL YOU DOUBT,
> AND SHE GOES OUT.
>
> EVERYTHING'S DIFFERENT,
> NOTHING'S CHANGED,
> ONLY MAYBE SLIGHTLY
> REARRANGED.

YOU'RE SORRY-GRATEFUL,
REGRETFUL-HAPPY,
WHY LOOK FOR ANSWERS WHERE NONE OCCUR?
YOU ALWAYS ARE WHAT YOU ALWAYS WERE,
WHICH HAS NOTHING TO DO WITH,
ALL TO DO WITH HER.

YOU'RE ALWAYS SORRY,
YOU'RE ALWAYS GRATEFUL,
YOU HOLD HER THINKING, "I'M NOT ALONE."
YOU'RE STILL ALONE.
YOU DON'T LIVE FOR HER,
YOU DO LIVE WITH HER,
YOU'RE SCARED SHE'S STARTING TO DRIFT AWAY,
AND SCARED SHE'LL STAY.

GOOD THINGS GET BETTER,
BAD GET WORSE.
WAIT—I THINK I MEANT THAT
IN REVERSE.

YOU'RE SORRY-GRATEFUL,
REGRETFUL-HAPPY,
WHY LOOK FOR ANSWERS WHERE NONE OCCUR?
YOU'LL ALWAYS BE WHAT YOU ALWAYS WERE,
WHICH HAS NOTHING TO DO WITH,
ALL TO DO WITH HER.

YOU'LL ALWAYS BE WHAT YOU ALWAYS WERE,
WHICH HAS NOTHING TO DO WITH,
ALL TO DO WITH HER.
NOTHING TO DO WITH,
ALL TO DO WITH HER.

The point of view, in sum, takes form as a kind of camera angle. A case of this in my workshop is inversely illuminating. To provide some extra practice in collaboration, one of the members proposed making a class project of adapting *Alice in Wonderland* into a musical. She would set up the entire book, different scenes of which would be divided among different workshop teams of collaborators, trying the opening scene herself, including lyrics. The proposal was welcomed, and we started. The point of view problem got in the way immediately.

How did everyone see *Alice in Wonderland*? In the original, where is the viewpoint? Is it through Lewis Carroll, through Alice, or through the White Rabbit? Is it down the rabbit hole, through the looking glass, dream? Is it in the reader? Does it differ if the reader is an adult or a child? If they read it together? The child's imagination leaps, but where does the adult's go: does he start seeing "meanings," which stop his imagination? And so on.

The organizer-bookwriter-lyricist came up with an original answer. She saw the musical as a giant chess game, in which each scene would take place as a different move on the chessboard. This unified all views, and seemed to be a provocative idea. The next step was to move from the abstract to the concrete, to an actual, changing chessboard stage. But the originator could not take this step, preferring to keep the viewpoint a *concept*, held only in her mind, not set before the audience's eyes. Arguments boiled over, we foundered, and the project was lost. Make that concrete step.

Sum: Style

The style of the musical is the sum of all these root components. The moment of starting with *seed* anticipates it. The way of crystallizing *story* concentrates it. *Spirit* amplifies it, and *sound and look* embody it. *Point of view* solidifies it. *Style* arrives in every way these are allowed to work as tools.

Every piece of work that fulfills the reality unique to it achieves style; *unique reality* is style in action. Style does not come last, a mannerism to lay over as a gloss. The perfecting of all art is not *a* style but style itself, the unique reality fulfilled, or in Stark Young's words, content perfectly expressed.

Realizing style is from the start the very heart of the work, the expression of its necessity. Write a letter to Macy's or to a friend, and the different style of each comes immediately, and all the way through. Extended to making theater, the style of a particular work is just as naturally and totally its unique reality, and what makes real in art, makes new.

Book, then, is book, music and lyrics *all together*. It does not matter that they are singled out in the trade by custom and in these pages for convenience. All develop out of the root elements of this chapter. There are problems ahead in any musical collaboration, but the worst ones may be avoided and many others eased by having taken full time for such first steps as these.

The Implements of the Book

Action
Character
Situation
Time and Place
Dance
Dialogue
Sum: Plot

The principal implements for dramatizing musical theater are the next steps of the book as *lead sheet*. Clearly these are also the songwriters' business as much as the bookwriter's. It is everyone's job to determine what a song should do and say, and where it fits; even more, out of what it comes and to what it leads. In other words, how a song may take over plot points "to compress and enlarge" them has only a collaborative answer; for a musical, two heads, or three, are better than one. The more demanded of him in total, the more each specialist may surpass himself. The ideal result is everyone's best ideas and skills made one.

Fear no fights in the process; there will not be very much of a show without them. Nothing will have mattered enough. The only hazard is a bad fight—the collision merely of egos. A good fight is one in which each collaborator finds out exactly what he means, and if he means it.

25

Action

Action is the most basic dramatizing tool of all. It is what propels the show from beginning to end. There is more to a show than its action, but there is no show at all without an action.

First, however, two uses of the word are excluded. Action here means *intention*, it does not mean physical motion or violence, as in chase or fight scenes. Nor does it refer to pieces of *business*, physical activities such as crossing the stage or embracing someone or handling props. The central meaning is: to take action.

"Actions speak louder than words." They reveal character. One mother runs into the street to save her child from a moving automobile, then spanks the child and screams, "Why did you do that?" Another runs out, grabs the child to her breast, bursts into tears, and pleads, "Why did you do that?" A third runs out, pulls the child away, and then calmly asks, "Why did you do that?" Exactly the same situation, exactly the same words, but three very different women, because of three very different actions: to scold, to beg, to reason. Action is character. A single actress, playing the three different actions, would also emerge as three different characters. To create and develop a character, *mark and reveal his actions.*

An action must "take place." It becomes visible to an audience only when it seeks *to overcome a problem.* If a man offers to shake another man's hand while you are watching, and the second man simply accepts it, the handshake occurs but does not take place: you will not necessarily see it. If the second man resists, however, and the first seizes his hand anyway, you cannot miss it. This is a *dramatic action.* In overcoming resistance, the action becomes visible: "take place" is literally the right phrase. *Drama*, from the Greek, means "a thing done."

Actions, the concrete drives that human needs turn into, are as familiar or extraordinary or grotesque as the catalogue of humankind. Dramatically, they are always pitted against difficulty and resistance. There is no balcony scene without Romeo being in danger, no garden scene without Gwendolyn and Cecily thinking they are rivals for the same man. Confronting conflicts within themselves or between each other, characters reveal each other, and relay the story out front to the audience.

Every show will thus have a main action that propels it. Its importance is central: it defines all the individual character actions. Here are different ways to find a show's main action.

What, or who, drives the sequence of situations forward, or brings everything together? (This is sometimes the main action of the main character: Oedipus, Hamlet, St. Joan, Blanche in **A Streetcar Named Desire**. In musicals: Nellie in **South Pacific**, Rose in **Gypsy**, Tevye in **Fiddler on the Roof**, Candide.)

What is the need that compels all other needs?

What is the stake? (What difference does it make to win or lose it?)

In "Method" vocabulary, what is the *through line, super-objective* or *spine* of the show?

What is the conflict, or central tension, that the writers must make sure to keep going? (This is a practical translation of the previous ones.)

Since these are only different forms of the same question, it does not matter which one is taken up. The answers come out the same. If none is fruitful, however, there is another way.

If the *story* was caught sharply enough, the main action is already there, in the key of the verb.

Story of **My Fair Lady**: A man transforms a girl, and *vice versa*.
The main action: To make Eliza into a "lady" (which she may have been all the while, without the accessories) and Higgins into a "gentleman" (which he is not, despite the accessories).
Story of **Company**: Bachelor tests out friends.
The main action is Robert's main action: To test out friends.

These *story main actions* will lead Higgins, Eliza and Robert into all their encounters, or situations. In other words, *character main actions* will stem from them, and so will all .the subsidiary actions into which a main action splits in specific situations (sometimes called *unit* or *specific* actions). If a blank occurs in determining specific actions, incidentally, falling back on his character main action will keep the character going.

To discover and execute actions is the aim of all dramatizing, and of all the tools incident to it. For action is what *relates* characters to each other, and forms the matrix of drama. Were one able to watch secretly, a person alone in a room might reveal a little of what he is like after awhile, but two people will reveal infinitely more instantly. Character shows most deeply in relationships.

For the writer, dramatic actions are *concrete verbs* of relating. Putting them into infinitives is the easiest way to make sure the verbs express character in forms not only transitive but *actable*. It also ensures keeping "meanings" out of actions in the same way they need to be kept out of *story*. Meanings are the *results* of actions—what we make of what others do, the audience's part, not the writer's. The control here is a master one: obey the character's needs only, never the author's. This is hard to apply, as in setting the point of view, but everything else, from subplot to subtlety, will hang on it.

One subtlety is substantial. Actions "fail"—an outcome that need not confuse but prove to be an advantage. Most of the great dramatic actions fail. Blanche is not trying to go insane, she is trying to keep her sanity. Oedipus carries through the action that dooms him, Hamlet pursues an action that destroys him, Alceste pursues one that betrays him, only Edmund (Eugene) of all the Tyrones (O'Neills) finds a way to survive, and General St. Pé, Willy Loman, George and Martha, Billy in **Carousel**, Rose in **Gypsy** and Charity all persist in actions that defeat them. In real life, we can never know the outcome of an action. It is exactly what makes us keep trying, sometimes harder and harder. The dramatist may know in advance that the character will "lose" or "fail." The inexperienced or unthinking dramatist subconsciously applies this knowledge, however, so that he weakens or, worse, rejects the very action that will most define the character. Actions succeed sometimes, but the ones that fail, getting into more and more difficulty, tragic or comic, may be the deepest ones.

There is one other distinction to make—between what may be called a *story action* and a *character action*. The former is the deceptive one, the latter the desired one, by which to dramatize.

In the example above of the three mothers, all shared the same story action, to save the child. Their different actions in doing so are what gave them their characters. Similarly, Hamlet and Laertes both share the same story action, to avenge their fathers. Again, the action each pursues in going about it reveals their different characters. It cannot be repeated too much that *revealing* character through action, not recounting it, is the aim. Thus, "to tell" or "to explain" are never character actions, nor "to convince" or "to persuade," or similar generalities. *How* a character does such things are the keys to his identity. The story action is always there, the actor must enter or exit, but the character action makes the difference.

In musicals, the action is the springhead of the songs. The basic definition of a show song is that it is a *heightened action.* As such, a song may start an action, advance it, bring it to a peak, or all these things at once, and thereby create or advance character. Similarly, to further character inevitably forwards the action. Two similar situations, one from **Guys and Dolls** and the other from **Carousel,** will illustrate.

The first romantic song in **Guys and Dolls** is "I'll Know," a duet between unlikely lovers, Sarah Brown, the Salvation Army sergeant, and Sky Masterson, the hot-shot Broadway gambler. On a bet, Sky is trying to make a date with Sarah, but is getting nowhere. And the action is slowing down. Keeping Sky at bay, Sarah begins the verse of the song. Before she gets through four lines, however, Sky interrupts and begins to undermine her defenses. She retorts with the affirmation of the first chorus. He then usurps the second chorus, and turns it upside down against her, breaking through into a new action. The conflict re-mounts afresh.

"If I Loved You," in **Carousel,** offers a serious parallel to the comic "I'll Know." It is also the first meeting of unlikely lovers, a duet between the patient home-town girl, Julie Jordan, and the rough carousel barker, Billy Bigelow. The man this time is baffled, while the girl knows exactly what is going on. This time he starts the song. She sits there. He begins with a partial reprise of the song, "You're a Queer One," the same thing that Carrie, Julie's best friend, called her. Julie answers Billy, but no more than she answered Carrie. The song innovatively turns into a verse introducing a new, richer song. Julie lifts the music into "If I Loved You," then leaves it to Billy to take over and follow through the idea. Again a relationship takes a crucial step.

Then, in the section beginning, "There's a helluva lot o' stars in the sky," they "trade" each other's characters, a sign of falling in love, as Billy assimilates the kinship with the natural universe which comes so easily to Julie. The newness of the experience captures him; and his surrender is inevitable. Throughout the scene, in addition, there is an inter-mix of spoken dialogue and underscoring, dialogue turning into song, song sometimes hesitant and partial. But full song always takes over when it should and the music underneath never stops. The method made **Carousel** a *dramatic operetta.*

Both examples demonstrate cardinal principles. The moment has to be high enough to want song, and a good song develops into an action that spoken words cannot equal.

With well-chosen actions, every development is heightened, and every heightening is a possibility for song. Starting, finishing or having trouble with a show, the first solution is the action.

Character

The main action of each individual character comes from the stake each has in the main action of the entire show. Here are some musical samplings of main character actions (and therewith, main songs).

> Main action of **My Fair Lady**: To make Eliza into a "lady"— and Higgins into a "gentleman."
>
> Main action of Higgins: To prove his power. ("Why Can't the English?," "I'm an Ordinary Man" and "A Hymn to Him")
> Eliza: To get her due. ("Wouldn't It Be Loverly?," "Just You Wait!" and "Without You")
> Doolittle: To get his slice of "the main chance." ("With a Little Bit of Luck")
> Freddy: To worship womankind (in transformed Eliza). ("On the Street Where You Live")
> Colonel Pickering: To put a master on his mettle. ("You Did It!")
>
> Main action of **Company**: To test out friends.
>
> Main action of Robert: To test out his friends. ("Someone Is Waiting" and "Being Alive")
> Joanne (the most often married): To keep trying, against her experience, for lovers. ("The Ladies Who Lunch")
> Amy (the girl Robert comes closest to marrying): To flee enough to get caught. ("Getting Married Today")
> Marta (the "kook-intellectual" of the single girls): To play tag and never be It. ("Another Hundred People")

The *turned-out spirit* of musical theater has another and far-reaching effect on creating character. Characters "turn out" also, a method that musicals share with Shakespeare, already noted as kin. All characters appear clear and full-blown on sight. On first entrance, Sir John is immediately Falstaff, Harry Percy is Hotspur, Katherine is Kate, however more they will develop. So is Harold Hill the music man, Joey pal Joey, Charity sweet Charity, right away. In contrast to the gradual character disclosure of realistic theater, referred to as "onion-peeling," character development in musical theater might be called, to coin a word, "beanstalk-springing." In the former, character is dense: packed, detailed, in grays, color to come. In the latter, character is sharp: line-drawn, contoured, in color to start. Both will forward character, but minutely in the former, boldly in the latter; recognition in the former will come on the last exit, in the latter, on the first entrance. "Beanstalk-springing" gains enormous time in a musical, to make room of course for the music.

If a musical character does turn "private," he does so again à la Shakespeare, not to retreat into himself but to re-connect with the world around him. Brilliant examples are Billy's "Soliloquy" in **Carousel**, "Rose's Turn" in **Gypsy**, "I've Grown Accustomed To Her Face" in **My Fair Lady** and "Being Alive" in **Company**. "Musical soliloquies" have been so overused that some experienced writers avoid them now on principle. They are dangerous and difficult to write, but the good ones are eminent and varied, as the following brief chronological list shows.

"Ol' Man River," **Show Boat**
"Bewitched, Bothered and Bewildered," **Pal Joey**
"Lonely Town," **On the Town**
"A Puzzlement," **The King and I**
"Pirate Jenny," **The Threepenny Opera**
"Joey, Joey, Joey," **The Most Happy Fella**
"Something's Coming," **West Side Story**
"Much More," **The Fantasticks**
"What Kind of Fool Am I?", **Stop the World,**
　　I Want to Get Off
"Ice Cream," **She Loves Me!**
"Who Are You Now?", **Funny Girl**
"Where Am I Going?, **Sweet Charity**
"If He Walked Into My Life," **Mame**
"Whoever You Are," **Promises, Promises**

All these songs are high spots of their shows, and all without exception turn in to turn out. There is a contrary list of failures, however, which is obviously innumerable. They fail because instead of attacking the problem in which the character finds himself, they lament it, which stops the action and puts off the audience. A good soliloquy seeks something for the character to do about the problem, which advances the action and enlists the audience. Though there are few good soliloquies, it is frequently one of the first songs young writers attempt. It should be one of the last, when the ability to employ actions that *relate* characters, that turn them out, is mastered.

Indeed, the first songs to write are those of the main characters in their main onstage confrontations, so far as they may be known, and with no concern for sequence. Central ideas in both content and style will define themselves this way. One of the advantages of musical theater is that it spells out the rhythms that actions take. To discover characters, discover their songs.

What might such rhythms be? The tool of *sound and look* may serve to essentialize character also. In the sharpest, most imagistic words applicable, even if some have to be invented, pick up the *sound* of each character, and each one's characteristic *movement* and gesture. Again, some **My Fair Lady** and **Company** models:

Sound	Movement

HIGGINS (Character action: To prove his power)

roars and growls	trampling and bull-dozing
whines, coaxings and	chest-thumps and foot-stamps
bullyings	petting, scratching and
hmphs, bahs and baas	fussing
	sulking in his tent
	letting go (at last)

ELIZA (To get her due)

howls, squeaks and coos	from awkward exaggerations
shrieks, flourishes and	to beautiful balances
rhapsodies	
chortles, chuckles and purrs	

DOOLITTLE (To get his slice of "the main chance")

schemings, clacks, boasts	nose-thumbing and floor-
retorts, banterings,	scraping
grandiloquences	swaggering and squirming
	capering and posing
	dodges and pounces

FREDDY (To worship womankind [in transformed Eliza])

praises and serenades
pledges, giggles, gramercies

prostrations and cloud-leaps
bended knees, services,
    gift-bearings
pedestal-raisings and
    idolatries

PICKERING (To put a master on his mettle)

courtesies and dares
toasts and cheers

bows, pats and prods
salutes, usherings
refereeing, standing by

ROBERT (To test out friends)

from scoffs and sighs of
    watchful waiting and
    secret wanting
to ahems and amens of giving
    in and taking hold

from watcher to doer
from passing by to standing
    up to jumping in
to on his own

JOANNE (To keep trying, against her experience, for lovers)

brassiness, brays, quacks
quips, dry sobs, damnations

advances, retreats
winks and waves
traffic-directing, attention-
    getting

AMY (To flee enough to get caught)

gasps, coughs and spatters
protests, entreaties
rants, racings
avowals

thrashings, frozen stares,
    grasps
scurryings, besiegings
riding throughs

MARTA (To play tag and never be It)

a siren, a whisper
sneers, snorts, snickers
    and crowings
jeremiads and hosannas

a come-on, a stand-off
one to one, one to many
sparring, shadow-boxing,
    change partners and dance
    with me

In this listening-in to and catching sight of the characters, let them steer, too; they have more to tell the writer than the writer knows. Having sensed their rhythms, their songs may also come nearer. This will include the characters interacting, sometimes taking on the songs of others, singly, together, for, against. Songs so discovered begin to trace each character's development, and major moments and developments marshal themselves. More songs than eventually used will doubtless result, but so much the better. They will provide an abundance of suggestions to plot from, turn a chore into a sport, and against the future strains and stresses of rehearsal and tryout will even provide a reserve of ideas to turn to, when changes are urgent.

The following examples from **My Fair Lady** and **Company**, though finished results, illustrate how this works out:

HIGGINS

An egomaniacal phonetics expert into, precisely, a staccato speak-singer.

In quality so intense, in vocation so expert, his character builds through songs in increasing explosions: "Why Can't the English?," "I'm an Ordinary Man," "You Did It!," "A Hymn to Him" (WHY CAN'T A WOMAN. . . ?).

Then, climax song, a complete change-over: "I've Grown Accustomed to Her Face." Eliza has gotten to Higgins by this point: his tune changes to hers, his most lyrical song.

ELIZA

Two kinds of songs: lyrical on her own, then under Higgins influence, more spoke-sung. "Wouldn't It Be Loverly?" jumps to "Just You Wait", switches back to "I Could Have Danced All Night", leaps into belting, lyrical-spoken combination, "Show Me!"

Finally, climax song, "Without You." Eliza outdoes Higgins' tune.

In addition, the two climax songs climax the story. The transformations of both Higgins and Eliza are proven out: the show's main action is completed.

DOOLITTLE

Two songs only, "before" and "after": "With a Little Bit of Luck" and "Get Me To the Church on Time." From "honest workingman" to "middle class morality," likewise "transformed" by the show's main action.

More, both are group songs led by him, jester-king of his rowdy crowd.

FREDDY

Perfectly, one song only: "On the Street Where You Live," and solo only: a serenade. The worshipful, romantic, very tenor to the life. Does little else but sing; once started, never seems to stop. Counter-action against main action of transforming.

PICKERING

Appropriately, no solos, but supports; two songs: "The Rain in Spain" and "You Did It!" Former already noted as a major turning-point; latter, peak from which final complications and resolutions unroll.

ROBERT

Character compacted through songs of increasing sharpness, from detachment to involvement: solo "Someone Is Waiting;" ensemble number with all the marrieds, "Side by Side by Side/What Would We Do Without You?"; duet with single girl friend, "Barcelona." Titles alone almost tell the story.

The climax song, and the musical's: "Being Alive," solo against entire company. Apparent "surrender," coincidentally like Higgins', but similarly revealing coming to maturity—independence finding commitment.

Overall: Testing out friends, Robert's main action, is also the show's; and every song in it dramatizes it, single and group. For individual examples:

JOANNE, AMY, MARTA

Each only one solo, though extensive: "The Ladies Who Lunch," "Getting Married Today," "Another Hundred People." Each, however, forms core of scenes built completely out of them—song paragons of character essentialization.

The easy labels of *soprano, baritone, leading man* or *soubrette (comedy ingenue)* have long faded. Songs, the rhythms of actions, are the developments of character, which lace the musical together. Character is destiny to the philosopher, but it is plot to the dramatist.

Situation

Every story starts from a *situation*, every action is a response to one. Sometimes the situation is central and its developments radiate like spokes (**Company, Fiddler on the Roof**). Sometimes it is initial and sets up progressive situations (**My Fair Lady, Hello, Dolly!**). In either case, *situation* is what prods character actions.

A situation is a conflict in human relationships—at bottom a lack of relationship—between individuals trying for something. This includes the probability that the relationship may collapse or explode, which is exactly what to use, not reject. It is what makes it dramatic. Comedy or tragedy, the stake in all situations should be as personal and high-pressured as possible.

Putting concrete "names" to such situations helps execute this; the more metaphorical, the better. Movie and TV teasers, for instance, offer familiar characterizations of such *set-ups*. Westerns: "A former gun-fighter arrives in Dodge City." To dramatize that, "Threat to peace." Or, "Danger! Dynamite." Situation comedies (note the name of the genre): "Teen-age daughter meets a new boy friend." Translations, "True Love—again." Or, "Stand back. Volcano!" Or, "Gidget rides again!"

In **My Fair Lady**, whose overall situation might be termed, "The battle of the classes and the sexes," the initial situation might be, "On the barricades," or, "Fat cats and alley cats." It is brought to a head by the character drives of the two leading characters, Professor Henry Higgins and flower-girl Eliza, out of their life actions crossing at that moment. These drives are epitomized by the musical's first two character songs, "Why Can't the English?" and "Wouldn't It Be Loverly?." They make the collision of Higgins and Eliza inevitable.

In **Company**, the situation staying throughout is literally "surprise party." Since it is specifically the occasion of the leading character's 35th birthday, some names for it might be, "Milestones make millstones," or, "Rite of passage," or, "Inventory," or, "Marriage-go-round and single-go-round." It is also musically epitomized by the entire-cast number, "Company," which precipitates the opening scene, and every development thereafter. (The complete lyrics may be found beginning on page 123.)

In short, a dramatic situation proves itself by triggering other situations. As a result, there will now be *scenes*. For working methods, scenes may be divided one from the other by every single entrance and exit, as the French do; *French scenes* make sure that every arrival and departure makes a difference. Or they may be divided by every change of time or place. Either way must make each change count.

Incorporate every moment that will heighten each scene, by build or by contrast, rhythm and counter-rhythm. As a story turns on one chief event, so does every scene turn on one single sub-event, or series of them, and each in turn pivots on *single moments*. A scene may thus be one situation coming to a head, or a succession of situations coming to a head. A set of such scenes, mounting, is a show.

Equally paramount is the requirement that situations trigger actions. Once a situation or difficulty is "named," what the characters *want* to do about it will likely produce their character actions. This is an alternate, by the way, to deriving them from the *story* main action.

What does Higgins want to do about the "battle of the British classes and the sexes?" He wants *to prove his power*. What does Eliza want to do about it? She wants what's coming to her, *to get her due*. From the character's viewpoint, it should be added, the situation may differ. Higgins' version of the situation might be: "challenge;" Eliza's: "sudden chance." The process applies the same, the actions come out the same.

What does Robert want to do about the "surprise party?" He wants *to put it to the test* of what his commitments are, and his friends'. His personal situation might be: "drifting cut short!". He still puts that to the test.

This is only a return to the basic definition of a dramatic action: to overcome a problem. The situation is that problem—or, the object of the action. Since the most pragmatic use of an action is its power to *relate* characters, the most important next step is to make sure the action has an object. The best dramatic objects are other human beings. Higgins wants to prove his power over everyone, but especially *over Eliza;* Eliza wants her due from everyone, but especially *from Higgins;* Robert wants to test his commitments and his friends' commitments, and he proceeds to do so *with each one*.

From character actions, plots develop freely. When Eliza's challenge takes hold, it proves Higgins' undoing; getting her due from Higgins, what he owes her keeps growing. When Robert finds that commitment may mean sharing his life, it also puts him more in charge of it.

The instinct for situation, accordingly, is a major dramatic power; musical theater facilitates it even more so. The dynamic kinds of places which *open up* the story to music and dance automatically foster a liveliness and variety of situations; this also liberates plotting. The pitfall is failing to *complete* the *given* moment. All the particularities that fit and further it must be realized. Rushing through, lack of attention to or lack of appreciation of all that the moment contains, are some of the traps. The costs range from superficiality to muddles to impasses. A worse mistake is the temptation to make a point. Its cost is to stop the action: precisely for having interrupted, the point cannot be made; points, above all, must be ingrained. Effects must have their causes.

Implementing a situation completely is highly demanding, and only actual practice teaches what traps to avoid and coups to score. It is in fact the heart of the work, to which everything in this chapter points.

Time and Place

Time and *place* are other circumstances of *situation,* the *setting* of the scene. But there are specifics to them that count even more.

Time is era and season as well as hour, *place* is culture and environment as well as site. *Period* is anything not the present; these are the only times and places in the theater. Without a single word change, a scene at eleven in the morning in the kitchen is a different scene from one at eleven at night in the bedroom. Eleven o'clock is different 100 and 1,000 years ago, in Rome and Romania.

They cannot indeed be defined separately from each other. They fix our sense of location between them; without them, we could not function. They may even suggest a state of mind: Siam then or New York now, or Brigadoon every hundred years, or Camelot, or Never-Never Land. They may also evoke states of being: "April in Paris," "September Song." More practically, time and place subject us, dictating every specific of our behavior: what we wear, how we move, even how we talk; nothing that we do is ever isolated from the time and place we do it in.

But besides setting scenes, time and place are distinct ways to maximize *situation.* Dramatically conjoined, they heighten scenes enormously. Dramatically contrasted, they create new scenes of their own. "Tonight" in **West Side Story** counterpointed time and place in one scene, as **I Do! I Do!, Hair** and **Company** did in entire shows. These were cited earlier, for the gains in character development in each case. A different application is **Gypsy.**

A passage of time had to be telescoped early in the musical by a jump of several years. A vaudeville song-and-dance routine is under way, "Baby June and Her Newsboys," to the tune of "Let Me Entertain You," established at the opening. The jump was made by keeping the place (a vaudeville stage) the same, but rearranging both the routine and the tune before our eyes. The children in the "newsboy" act are in red, white and blue. Halfway through, the tempo picks up, the orchestra amplifies, and a flashing stroboscope light begins. To various forms of *trenches* (or *traveling*), the tap dance step that looks like running, the children are replaced one by one by their grown-up counterparts, in the same costumes. (In *trenches*, the body leans forward, the arms hang and swing, and long, gliding footsteps are taken rapidly. In profile, the step is called *chases*, because the dancers look as if they are catching, passing and re-passing each other. Used for *false exits* when it nears the wings, it was used here for actual actor substitutions.)

The compression of time scored an instant point. Under their mother's dominance, June and her sister Louise (Gypsy), now in their teens, are still doing a "baby" act. Apart from its theatrical excitement, the number heightens the action because as a reprise it exposes that the family is getting nowhere, and primes the audience for something to burst. Indeed, the leitmotif use of "Let Me Entertain You" throughout the musical produced major character advances each time. First introduced in "cutesy" waltz time, it returned in this scene in tinny, fast time, then mounted thematically in and out of other situations, and even other songs. At the moment when Gypsy "breaks through" in burlesque, it appeared in the biggest reprise of all, a driving, four-beat-to-the-bar striptease number, to provide the turning point of Act II; then it echoed one last time in the remarkable climax song that follows, "Rose's Turn."

The variety possible in such use of a song does not merely compress but ignites plot developments. It does so by how much time in place, or places in time, it can cover. Music, swifter and stronger than words alone or a scenic change, by counterpointing time and place, recharges them.

Another particular use of time-place opportunities is physical, rather than musical and choreographic. **I Do! I Do!** employed a theater convention called *limbo*, in this case the runway. *Limbo* is any stage area which is no place in general so that on order it may become a place in particular. A show as a whole may take place in limbo, on a bare stage set only with minimum needs. While modern dance, under Martha Graham's influence, offers the most obvious examples, some musicals *in limbo* include **The Fantasticks, Roar of the Greasepaint, Hair, Celebration, Your Own Thing, You're a Good Man, Charlie Brown** and **Zorba.**

Company provides a special example. In contrast to **Gypsy** or **I Do! I Do!,** the place changes, but the time does not. It is, in fact, frozen around the moment of waiting for Robert's arrival in his apartment for his surprise birthday party. The moment is established at the beginning, returns in the middle and closes the musical. It is otherwise fragmented into all the places and relationships that have brought Robert to it—and that may issue from it. To take us anywhere instantly, therefore, the stage was made into another kind of limbo, a *unit set.* In a unit set, the overall frame of the design remains constant, but insert elements are changed within it. In **Company**, as an expressionist abstraction of chrome steel elevator platforms rose and descended, and various set-pieces were swiftly tracked in and out, places came and went within one time-envelope. This was musical theater's venture into absurdist theater storytelling: a single situation spiralling around itself, instead of linear situations progressing forward. Part of the vitality of the American musical is ceaselessly to pioneer.

On the musical stage, reality breaks out of naturalistic time and place, to lift, not lock, the show. For the time of musical theater is the high, swift "two hours' traffick" across it, not the dwelling within it, and the place of musical theater is the stage itself, greeting the audience directly.

Dance

The part of musical theater that lifts it the highest of all, and most actively denies the literal, is dance. As already noted, dance is often the animating force of a show. There is a French proverb, "What can be spoken can be sung, what can be sung can be danced." Musicals like **Carousel, West Side Story, Pippin** and **A Chorus Line** are spectacular applications of how much dance may dramatize. Musical theater writers need not be informed of the techniques of dance, but they need very much to be informed by its spirit. There are some show writers whose verbal and musical powers are great, yet who are unaware or even afraid of dance's powers. Dance is supplemental for them, and what it accomplishes, a surprise. This is to miss how much an asset a *sense* of dance can be in creating a musical.

The forms of theater dance are several: classic ballet, modern dance, jazz, ethnic and folk, tap, ballroom, acrobatic, exotic—and a mixture of any of these. All, however, serve only one of two purposes: to tell a story, or to express pure movement. In musical theater, the second purpose, if used, serves the first. A great part of a choreographer's experience teaches him to tell a story in dance. Accordingly, he becomes a co-author to be accepted, even welcomed, for a capacity to make sharp contributions to the script as a whole. This does not mean that writers should expect to devise dance "scenarios" in any detail; on the contrary, that is to be avoided, left to the expert. It does mean availing themselves of the storytelling potentials of dance. There are several, as follows.

Dance can *condense* and *telescope* better than many songs, and any dialogue:

Two collaborators in my workshop, a bookwriter-lyricist and a composer, working on adapting Dreiser's *Sister Carrie* into a musical drama, were having difficulty with the Act II opening. The point had been reached where Carrie and her married lover, Hurstwood, had run off to New York. This would be the peak of their happiness; from there on the action would dive to the final curtain.

The writers began with a domestic scene of arrival in the lovers' flat, with a gay song in the middle for Carrie about "A Can of Peaches," their first "dinner." Neither the scene nor the song was getting off the ground. They tried stretching time in the scene, adding dialogue sections around encores of the song, with lyric changes as the affair began to fall off. The scene was still too small and too literal, and the act opening was not coming to life.

It took months before they found it. They wrote a different song, and obeyed a choreographic instinct. The setting was changed to a lamppost with street signs in an open space of two or three levels. Hurstwood now appeared rushing through the streets of New York from the financial district to the flat singing "Going Home to Carrie," and passing groups of other New Yorkers in motion, plutocrats, office workers, the poor, the derelict, who sang a downbeat counter-melody with counter-lyrics against Hurstwood's gay, upbeat song. As Hurstwood or the crowds brushed against the lamppost, it would revolve and the street signs would change, denoting the stages of his journey.

In the visual-musical interplay distinctive of musical theater, the number in one stroke telescoped time, played up dramatic contrasts, concentrated the drama by physically incorporating a badly missing element, the grinding New York environment, and planted the denouement (Hurstwood ends up among the derelict). The scene caught fire, the act was launched, and the vision was widened, by employing, not literally but in spirit, a dance sense.

Dance can *establish* situation faster and stronger, in more colors and with more liveliness:

There are eminent examples of this, such as "The Carousel Waltz" in **Carousel,** "The March of the Siamese Children" and "The Small House of Uncle Thomas" in **The King and I,** "Tradition" in **Fiddler on the Roof,** or "I Hope I Get It" in **A Chorus Line.** Fuller illustrations will appear in the specific treatment of *establishing* and *opening* numbers.

Dance can *enlarge* any given song:

Examples of this are probably the most diverse and numerous. For a few, there are "Fugue for Tin Horns" and "Luck, Be a Lady" in **Guys and Dolls,** "Once in Love with Amy" in **Where's Charley?,** "The Name's LaGuardia" in **Fiorello!,** "Let Me Entertain You" in **Gypsy,** "I'm a Brass Band" in **Sweet Charity,** "She Likes Basketball" in **Promises, Promises,** and throughout in **Two Gentlemen of Verona,** whose continuous dance vitality, sometimes free, sometimes strict, was a large part of its infectiousness.

Dance can extend any *unspoken* moment, as it can also *evoke* things beyond words:

This once included the dream ballet which has grown old-fashioned but not faded away, as proved by its fresh, direct-action use in "Tevye's Dream" in **Fiddler on the Roof.** There are also the "Tick-Tock" number in **Company,** and "The Music and the Mirror" in **A Chorus Line;** and further instances all through **Two Gentlemen of Verona,** for an overall musical comedy example, and **Man of La Mancha,** for an overall musical drama example.

Dance can uniquely *bridge,* or *relieve* or *comment:*

These functions have frequent uses, and they even dominate such shows as **I Do! I Do!, Cabaret, Promises, Promises, Company** and **Pippin.** In **A Chorus Line,** dance indeed turns into both the score and the underscoring of the show. These aspects will also be more particularly illustrated under *segues* (bridging), *underscoring* (underlining), and *relief and comment* numbers.

Dance can *take over* storytelling directly, the biggest use of all:

It can start an action or further it, climax action or resolve it, and in sum heighten action as much as song, and even more. Sometimes it can even solve a plot problem better than song can, and certainly better than dialogue can. Since "Slaughter on Tenth Avenue" in 1936 in **On Your Toes,** dance has done one or more of these things either at critical points (**Oklahoma!, Kiss Me, Kate, The King and I, Can-Can, The Music Man, Fiorello!, Grease**), or centrally (**Carousel, Brigadoon, West Side Story, Follies, Pippin, A Chorus Line**). In all these instances and others, the writing was fortified by a choreographer's characteristic contribution: co-authoring and storytelling.

It works best when writers bring a dance outlook to their musical in the first place. It is obvious that choreographer-directors like Jerome Robbins, Bob Fosse and Michael Bennett, who conceive musicals, will incorporate dance fundamentally, just as from the beginning a Ray Bolger or Gwen Verdon musical will feature dance. Integrating dance, especially in spirit, should be natural to all musicals, however, and to all musical writers. Dance momentarily frees us from gravity; to quote one of my workshop writers, it puts air under the show. It may also raise the roof.

Dialogue

A fundamental and fascinating question has been reached. What is the "balanced economy" of song, dance and dialogue appropriate to a particular musical? A partial guide may be the differences between types of musicals—musical comedy, musical drama, "Broadway opera," *et al.* Each collaborator also brings his personal answer. But the final solution must be everybody's answer, and unique to the material. Wrestling with these balances may be one way to new kinds of musicals.

It is dialogue's turn for consideration. The bookwriter has two jobs: to pull together everyone's ideas on paper, and to write the dialogue. The former ability may be acquired. The latter is a gift, to be no less developed by incessant sharpening of the ear and shaping words to be said, not read. There is no end to the number of scripts that read well but played badly.

Two of the hazards are *exposition*, and writing *on the nose*. The term *exposition* is a disastrous invention. *News*, not information, is what dialogue must aim to be, news to the characters, and in that way news to the audience—discovery and illumination. "Planting" exposition is always contrivance, because it serves the writers' motivations, not the characters'. In life, background material comes to the fore when rising pressures force it out. That is the model of how to make it count in the theater. Characters call it forth because it makes a difference at that moment.

Writing dialogue (or a song, for that matter) *on the nose* is another snare. *On the nose* is to spell out too literally or too obviously what is at stake. It uses up the idea, instead of connoting it. Again, it is an author's, not a character's way of speaking; stage dialogue works by texture and nuance and suggestion, out of characters contending. Writing dialogue patly, by bald statement or to serve preconceived results, shows the bones, and goes dead.

To start writing immediately is another mistake. Even with genius, something has to come before. Musical writers have an added advantage, each other's collaboration for fueling ideas. Out of these combined searches comes the private tuning in, to who the characters are, and what they are doing and finally each character's vocabulary—verbal, musical and physical. Good writers are their characters' stenographers.

As for the balance of dialogue against other elements, rhythm once more operates as master guide. Dialogue functions differently in a musical than in a straight play. Since music expands dramatic moments, dialogue condenses them. Songs in general will make the most developed statements, against which dialogue in general will seem closer to "telegrams," *figuratively* speaking. Dialogue may not give up all the meatier moments, but it more often serves as underpinning for musical and dance takeovers, or as links between them.

It is easy to call dialogue weaknesses "book trouble," but it is a feat to create or develop character in only thirty lines instead of three hundred. Dialogue must also generate its own energy and color to keep pace with the more physical song and dance moments; it cannot drop too far, or disregard the style. Most of all, unless it sets up the song or dance in precisely the right context, tone and instant, even a good number fails, whereas properly set up, a middling number succeeds. A bookwriter who can make the most of these very high skills is indeed an expert.

Trends change, also. In musical comedies, shows like **Hair** have a scarcity of dialogue, while shows like **Promises, Promises** have an abundance. Today's bookwriters like Neil Simon, Alan Jay Lerner, Arthur Laurents, Hugh Wheeler and others bid for substance and wit. In musical drama, dialogue is also enlarging itself. The "telegramatic" technique is shifting in general. **Fiddler on the Roof** makes one of the most successful mixes of comic and dramatic rhythms. It does not always read well, but it played, of course, famously. In **Company**, a short-joke rhythm is still employed, but so are longer-rhythm comic developments. Yet, because the scenes come short, fast and often, punctuated by brief and frequent musical inserts in and around them, the effect remains "telegramatic."

Abandoning this altogether may be alien to anything short of the play-with-music.

Within musical theater, nevertheless, new and more interwoven balances of song, dance and dialogue, and comedy and drama, may lead in the future to character expression that will .be uniquely developed and fulfilled. **A Chorus Line** may be a culmination of the integrated musical, or a step in a new direction. Its matrix is dance, flowing through monologue/dialogue and song, in the course of which the music stops only three times; its innovativeness is the way dance founds and frames all the words, words rise into song, and then song rises back into dance.

The never-ending questions, then, of the "balanced economy" of any musical is whether to use dialogue *or* song *or* dance for any given moment, or dialogue *and* song *and* dance combined in one way or another. In the first case, how to decide which moments in particular belong to each? There is certainly no single answer. Here, for instance, are two high moments not made into song.

At the climax of Act I in **Camelot**, King Arthur has just invested five new Knights of the Round Table, the last one Lancelot du Lac. Arthur has also recognized that Lancelot and Guenevere will be lovers. Alone, he measures out three "propositions": his love of Guenevere, his love for Lancelot and the new ideal of civilization of which he is King. By Excalibur, Arthur vows to carry on the Round Table, his only choice.

The scene is underscored, but does not break into song. Did keeping it spoken have something to do with **Camelot**'s particular "balanced economy" to stay a "musical drama," especially for the Act I curtain? Or with the specific *sequence* of songs? Or with the casting of a leading classical actor, Richard Burton, to "top" a song by verbal eloquence? Or with the ambition of a leading bookwriter-lyricist, Alan Jay Lerner, to "top" his lyrics by dialogue eloquence? Or something else, for other reasons thought sufficient?

The second moment is from **The Rothschilds.** In the middle of Act I, the father, Mayer Rothschild, is presenting his five sons to his benefactor, Prince William of Hesse. It is the family's opportunity to escape the ghetto. Mayer demonstrates how remarkably he has trained his sons to understand, in several national languages, international money. A fast-tempo, seven-part dialogue exchange ensues between the six Rothschilds and the Prince before whom they are lined up. The moment could have easily been raised into song. Instead, the song comes right after the Prince's consent and exit, and it is about something else: an impromptu celebration on being launched into the banking business, "Rothschild and Sons." But was a natural song moment passed by, for reasons again good and sufficient for the writers?

Such choices are the heart of the job. It would be beside the point to learn the actual reasons. Writers of new musicals must make choices for their own reasons. The outcome is a matter of Branch Rickey's definition of luck: "the residue of design."

Song and dance do not get *all* the "big moments," then. Occasions may arise when dialogue is the most "compressed-enlarged" solution; it is also possible that some moments may elude or defy musicalizing. Sometimes particular numbers may come too close together; other times it may seem better to avoid the emphasis that a song always injects; or to reserve song only for the highest moments of all—if they can always be guessed in advance. Rehearsal and tryout prompt other adjustments and corrections.

Nowadays, as a result, some musicals have more dialogue than ever before, others have more songs than the 15 or so that used to be standard, and a few have less. The pitfalls are two. Dialogue may end up with too many of the biggest moments, in place of songs; in that case, the show is no longer a musical. Second, and more fatal, if dialogue and song (or dance) both try to do the same job, there is no show of any kind; the dialogue plays through, the song only repeats, and the show stops dead. The exact proportion of song, dance and dialogue for any given musical is always unique.

This involves also the other option—combining song, dance and dialogue. How to decide which moments deserve combined treatment, and how to implement them? Again, a single answer is impossible.

All the considerations that comprise the *style* of the musical is one guide, of which "If I Loved You" in **Carousel** is a model. Or the needs of a particular moment along the way may dictate a combined approach, as in "Tevye's Dream" in **Fiddler on the Roof**, or "Poor Baby" and "Tick-Tock" in **Company**. Sometimes dialogue is simply inserted into songs (or dances) in quick asides or, more pointedly, quick shifts and transitions, occasionally extended to several brief exchanges. Song may in turn cut into dialogue in snatches, except that finally it must take over, if it is to be a song. Whatever the device, the principle is to further the strongest action of the scene, and this is easiest to do through the song. In essence, the song is what the scene is about.

To what degree does dialogue set up song and dance, and take back over from them? This is the most basic question of all, and requires *bridging* dialogue into and out of songs and dances, called *"lead-ins"* and *"lead-outs."* Those old lead-ins—"Let me tell you how beautiful you are," or "Here come the girls!"—are primitive or nostalgic now; *song cues* will not do any more. The trick in writing them, however, remains: how to avoid using up the song in the lead-in?

This is a variation of the *on the nose* hazard. The lead-in must not give away or turn into what the song will say or do. It must only hint or kindle the next step up, the song. Brief or extended, it must move forward, then stop just short of the song.

For models of lead-ins, **My Fair Lady** is a paragon. In one that will serve well, Professor Higgins says to Colonel Pickering:

> . . . I find that the moment I let a woman make friends with me she becomes jealous, exacting, suspicious and a damned nuisance. I find that the moment I let myself become friends with a woman, I become selfish and tyrannical. So here I am, a confirmed old bachelor, and likely to remain so. After all, Pickering, I'm an ordinary man . . .

But that is precisely what Lerner and Loewe do not do. The lead-in ends at "After all, Pickering." The line, "I'm an ordinary man," is the beginning (and indeed the title) of the song:

> I'M AN ORDINARY MAN
> WHO DESIRES NOTHING MORE . . .

From that the song grows. Otherwise it would have had no place to go, it would have been *written through*, killed, a repetition instead of an advance. In the performance, incidentally, the lead-in works even more subtly. *Music under* the dialogue, infiltrating the song, begins early during the speech. (The cue can usually be set only during rehearsals, subject to an actor's particular rhythm.) The line, I'M AN ORDINARY MAN, is actually spoke-sung, but by then the melody is full up in the orchestra, and by the following lyric line Higgins is clearly singing. In other words, the audience cannot tell where the lead-in ends and the song begins.

(Not that dialogue words cannot occasionally reappear in the lyric, but such cases are clearly exceptions, and must all the more not use up the song. After the triumphant moment of "The Rain in Spain," Higgins' housekeeper, Mrs. Pearce, tells them all they have been working too hard, and tells Eliza to go to bed. Repeating the words in order to dispute them, Eliza responds:

BED! BED! I COULDN'T GO TO BED!
MY HEAD'S TOO LIGHT TO TRY TO SET IT DOWN!
SLEEP! SLEEP! I COULDN'T SLEEP TONIGHT!
NOT FOR ALL THE JEWELS IN THE CROWN!

I COULD HAVE DANCED ALL NIGHT! . . .

Unless such exceptions also heighten, they are better avoided.)

To build dialogue for songs to cap is ticklish, thankless and a feat of its own.

Lead-outs may look easier. The best lead-out, as someone has said, is applause. A show song works, however, because it makes a difference, it produces a change of some kind. It should therefore have brought the characters—and the audience—to some new point when the song is over. Tyro bookwriters sometimes commit a stupefying error. They write dialogue in which they leave gaps for the song, but then continue the dialogue as if the song had never happened. This defeats the song and betrays what the lead-out should do: move on from what the song has accomplished. Follow-ups that comment on or recap the number are gratuitous, or worse, cute, and again clog the forward build. The next event, not the last, is all that matters. Lead-outs may of course make scene endings.

It is true that some numbers by exception may count for sheer diversion without affecting plot. Specialties or spectacle may be interpolated as their own excuse. In such cases, the lead-out needs to be all the stronger, to retrieve forward movement. After any and all numbers, press forward—indeed, lead out.

Sum: Plot

In practice, dramatic structure does not begin but arrives. Its components, already large, of action, character, situation, time and place, intertwined in song, dance and dialogue, turn *story* into *plot*. To help achieve the final shape, first a check list:

Seed kept? Story "opened up?"
Spirit caught? Sound and look translated?
Point of view clear?
Style realized?

Actions "take place?" Actions define character?
Characters make discoveries? (An essential way to
    dramatize.)

Situations provoke actions? Main events in the
    situations—"scenes?"
Most being made of time and place?

Situations build up conflicts? Detonate them?
Confrontations and showdowns along the way? High
    enough?
Solutions to conflicts often lead to new conflicts: apply?

Hints and plants set up for payoffs? Suspense long enough
    before payoffs? Enough surprises to cap payoffs?
Climaxes happening, small and big? Where distributed?
Resolved? Left open? (Latter more an option today.)

Absolutely nothing taken for granted? All assumptions filled
    in, all premises followed through? (Easy to miss, and fatal.)

Above all: song or dance take over action and character?
What shares in action and character given to what kinds of
    song, dance, dialogue?
Everything telling story? (If not, exceptions serve relevant
    purpose?)

To plot is not to plod. There are ways to renew imagination if it is
running down. Out of determining the story's main action, for instance, what *obstacles* may be thrown in its way? The more
obstructions, the more they may bring out the character actions to
overcome them.

In the first scene of **My Fair Lady**, outside the Royal Opera
House in Covent Garden, a series of quickening obstacles arise
from the very start: a confrontation of the "visiting" upper crust
with the "native" working class on a night that is cold and raining.
Through key character-establishing songs, out of interim growing
clashes, the strongest obstacles to each other, Higgins, and Eliza,
collide. Maintain high gear. Goad (challenge) the girl: bring her
and the man together again. Continue, inserting more obstacles.
Give the man, say, a "fatal flaw": he hates women. Put it into a
song, "I'm An Ordinary Man" (LET A WOMAN IN YOUR
LIFE. . . !). He charms the audience as his own worst enemy, even
as he whets its appetite for his comeuppance. Give the girl pride
and stubbornness of her own ("Just You Wait!"), and the audience
starts to root harder. Add the girl's father to get in everybody's way,
including his own "(With a Little Bit of Luck"). Build and build,

more obstacles in the path of more actions, until all that is left is the climactic resolution. Only bear in mind that one of the main differences between plotting musicals and plotting straight plays is that musicals require events which have *larger* details, and *fewer* details.

Another way to liberate plots is by the managing of time. A story may cover a long time, but its plot need only take a short time. There is a great deal of history before the audience meets Hedda Gabler or Willy Loman, but the plots occupy only the last two days of their lives. Three ways that musicals also "bring the past to a head" follow:

> Principal characters with conflicting histories meet for the first time, with instant consequences: **My Fair Lady, West Side Story, Guys and Dolls, Carousel, Promises, Promises, Brigadoon, Annie Get Your Gun, The Music Man, The King and I, Camelot, Showboat.**

> Principal characters are already involved in a relationship, with mounting consequences: **Company, A Little Night Music, Grease, Fiddler on the Roof, Hello, Dolly!, The Pajama Game, Kiss Me Kate, Porgy and Bess, Oklahoma!.**

> Principal characters arrive in exploding types or stages of relationships, with new consequences: **A Chorus Line, Raisin, Follies, Hair, Sweet Charity, The Fantasticks, Mame, Man of La Mancha, Celebration, The Medium.**

The jumping-off point, accordingly, can be many places. In musicals which cover longer periods, whose forms perilously turn episodic or *cavalcade*, the only control is to build around a strong central situation, as in **Gypsy** (mother and daughters) and **I Do! I Do!** (marriage crises), or **Candide** (separation) and **The Rothschilds** (ghetto barriers). But **The Rothschilds** shows the petard one may be hoist by in most such cases. Act I is Mayer's story, the founding father, but Act II turns into Nathan's, the son in England who is leader of the five brothers. A good musical might have been superlative, if it had stuck to one story instead of splitting into two. Time may also be treated not chronologically but in mixed fashion—sequences leaping back and forth to form a mosaic: **Hair** for one, **Follies** for another. Or time may be stopped, to extract and develop selected instants of it: **Promises, Promises** mildly, **Company** completely, and earlier examples under *sound and look* and *time and place*. Or juggling beginnings, middles and ends may suggest new orders of their own. Chronology or collage, time may be *composed* too. It is one of the strongest ways to make a plot *happen*. In all, however, the same questions apply. What special moments shall be the turning points? Are they placed where they work best?

An additional way to organize plot is an expansion of the lead-in/lead-out scheme. The general shape of most shows is a large curve, from lead-in up to the climax and lead-out. I ascribe to George S. Kaufman the dictum, "Get them up a tree in Act I. Throw rocks at them in Act II. Get them down in Act III." The pattern, not the division or the number of acts, is the point. Any one phase—up the tree, the rocks or getting down—may be the longest, or the shortest, including getting down in only the time it takes the final curtain to descend. In musicals today, the phases are customarily but not necessarily divided into two acts.

A subsidiary plotting aid has also been attributed to Kaufman: *shuffling.* He would write down the main events of each situation or scene on a card. Then he would shuffle them to discover a better order of scenes, or new connections between them. Kaufman was an exceptional card player, but the method is recommended no less. Another axiom is that if the end of a show is giving trouble, the beginning may be what is wrong. If there are "middle" problems, find new rocks or more rocks *(obstacles)* to throw. If difficulties still persist, go as far back to root ideas as *story*: it may not yet be right. Or, shuffle again.

There are shows, also, with *only* a middle nowadays: the one-situation plot that revolves around itself. This is an earmark of *existentialist* or *absurdist* theater, a single situation beginning and ending anywhere but spiraling around itself and going nowhere. It is also taken as a metaphor for contemporary life, of which **Waiting for Godot** is the obvious example. The musical theater has had its versions, too: one situation is the whole story, as in **Company.** Partial forms of it seem to be appropriate to rock musicals, such as **Hair, Salvation** and **Godspell.** Other musicals, like **Follies, Grease, Ain't Supposed To Die a Natural Death** and **A Chorus Line** have also adapted it.

In these cases, the suspense question becomes not how the situation will change, but how to sustain it without flagging. Open up all the facets in it that can be found. We do not wait for Lefty the way we wait for Godot. Plotting of suspense has run the gamut of extremes.

The plot, then, may be the direction a situation may go, or the form it may take. It is sometimes the cause but always the outcome of character responses to situation pressures. Trade character and situation back and forth. But lose one for the other, all too easy a slip, and the audience is lost.

If a *linear* plot is working, the audience wants to know what happens next. In a *non-linear* one, what happens now. Either way, *dramatic* plotting is not telling but revealing. Actions, as ever, speak louder than words. Let the audience discover and interpret them, and it has a part to play. Give the audience announcements, and it has none. Successful shows have parts for the audience, failures do not.

Refining the Book

The material has by now been brought to a certain level, through all attendant difficulties. The act of *refining* it represents that final perfecting, in essence never-ending, necessary to bring the material to its highest pitch.

All three craft aspects—book, music and lyrics—will each need to undergo it. But since music and lyrics are also book, this refining process will govern all subsequent aspects. Here, it is in two parts. The first furnishes some last tools to sharpen and round off the book work, and the second some closing considerations to facilitate and assess it.

Both should bring the bookwriting to contingent completion, armed for the concluding revisory bombardments that marketing, rehearsing and trying out the musical have in store.

Score

If the score of a musical is right, it not only integrates the plot, it goes so far as to confirm or correct it. Otherwise a score is only a collection of songs.

Two suppositions are in operation, that a number arrives at the main turning points of the plot, and that the plot is taking shape. The result will be that the *order* of numbers will constitute an outline of the plot. By themselves they form the spine of the musical.

Specifically, the *run-down* or *musical synopsis* shows whether the number is the right one, and in the right place. This includes the alternation of numbers—among the different characters, between solo and group members, and among kinds of numbers (*ballads, rhythm tunes, special material* and *production numbers*). It also suggests what plot points have been covered between numbers, whether such points are better served by a number or not, the amount of time between numbers, indeed the musical's entire "balanced economy," and similar practical check-outs.

Taking the run-down of **My Fair Lady** will demonstrate how a score serves as a musical's complete outline. It will be presented slightly expanded, to fill in each number's function in the plot—its action, stage setting and musical setting. **My Fair Lady** has 18 numbers and 4 reprises:

Place: London. *Time:* 1912.

ACT I

Scene 1: Outside the Opera House, Covent Garden. A cold March night.

1. "Street Entertainers"—*The 3 Buskers.* Establishes the "tug-of-war" worlds of the story.	Ensemble	Production Number
2. "Why Can't the English?" (see page 122)—*Higgins.* The male lead, proving his power.	Solo (with Ensemble)	Special Material
3. "Wouldn't It Be Loverly?" (see page 122)—*Eliza.* The female lead, wanting her due.	Solo (with Quartet)	Ballad

Scene 2: Tenement Section: Tottenham Court Road. Immediately following.

4. "With a Little Bit of Luck" (see page 126)—*Doolittle.* Eliza's father's "code": taking his cuts of the "main chance" where he's found them. An obstacle in everyone's way, the chief sub-plot.	Trio	Rhythm Tune

Scene 3: Higgins' Study. The following morning.

5. "I'm an Ordinary Man" (see page 140)—*Higgins.* Higgins the misogynist will "transform" Eliza, but certainly keep her out of his life. The main confrontation is under way.	Solo	Special Material

Scene 4: Same as Scene 2. Three days later.

6. "With a Little Bit of Luck": *Reprise* (see page 127)— *Doolittle.* With a half-chorus of his "theme song" with new lyrics, Doolittle jumps at a brand new main chance (Eliza has "moved in" with Higgins). The reprise advances character.	Ensemble	Rhythm Tune

Scene 5: Same as Scene 3. Later that day.

7. "Just You Wait!"—*Eliza.* Eliza protests Higgins' treatment. They are managing badly. Early next stage of the confrontation.	Solo	Rhythm Tune
8. "Poor Professor Higgins"— *Servants.* A continuing number, interspersed with dialogue sections, compressing the passage of time while elaborating Eliza's laborious progress.	Ensemble	Special Material
9. "The Rain in Spain"— *Higgins, Eliza, Pickering.* First success! The "transformation" takes. All join in to celebrate.	Trio	Rhythm Tune (also Special Material)

10. "I Could Have Danced All Night"—*Eliza*. Eliza rejoices, with a new-found feeling for Higgins. He danced with her.	Solo (with Svts.' Trio)	Ballad

(Scene 6: Near the Race Meeting, Ascot. A July afternoon.)
Two-page scene, no song.
Pickering arranges Eliza's
first "test" with Higgins'
mother.

Scene 7: Inside a Club Tent, Ascot. Immediately following.

11. "The Ascot Gavotte"—*Race Spectators*. Big "establishing number" shift. Sets in motion the testing of Eliza, and in its encore during the second race, detonates the climax of her "debut." ("Move your bloomin' arse!")	Ensemble	Production Number

Scene 8: Outside Higgins' House, Wimpole Street. Later that afternoon.

12. "On the Street Where You Live" (see page 128)—*Freddy*. All of a sudden, Eliza has a suitor, Freddy. In contrast to Higgins, he worships her.	Solo	Ballad

(Scene 9: Same as Scene 3. Six weeks later.)
Two-and-a-half page scene,
underscored but no song. Eliza
is dressed for the Ball.

(Scene 10: The Promenade of the Embassy. Later that night.)
Four-page scene, underscored
all through. The Big Test
begins.

Scene 11: The Ballroom of the Embassy. Immediately following.

13. "The Embassy Waltz"— *Higgins, Eliza, Karpathy, Guests*. Eliza—and Higgins— meet the Crucial Moment head on. Cliff-hanger. Curtain.	Ensemble	Production Number

ACT II

Scene 1: Same as Act I, Scene 3. 3:00 the following morning.

14. "You Did It!"—*Higgins, Pickering, Servants*. Lead-out: Celebration of the triumph at the Ball—with Eliza ignored.	Ensemble	Rhythm Tune
15. "Just You Wait!" *Reprise— Eliza*. This time Eliza's vow— with a slight change of lyrics, big change of class accent— truly threatens. The reprise advances character.	Solo	Rhythm Tune

Scene 2: Same as Act I, Scene 8. Immediately following.

16. "On the Street Where You Live": *Reprise—Freddy*. Pure Freddy still pursues, with the only song in him. But the reprise turns into a lead-in to:	Solo	Ballad
17. "Show Me!" (see page 145)— *Eliza*. Eliza's takeover response, blowing Freddy all over the street. From now on, she will clearly fend for herself.	Solo	Rhythm Tune

Scene 3: Flower Market of Covent Garden. 5:00 that morning.

18. "Wouldn't It Be Loverly?" *Reprise—Eliza*. Trying to join in on "her own" song, Eliza learns she can't go home again. The reprise advances character.	Solo (with Quartet)	Ballad
19. "Get Me to the Church on Time" (see page 127)—*Doolittle*. Doolittle's rousing farewell to the life he led, before he got his cut of the main chance that made him rich; his "after" song. Windup of the sub-plot.	Ensemble	Production Number

Scene 4: Upstairs Hall of Higgins' House. 11:00 that morning.

20. "A Hymn to Him" (see page 142)—*Higgins*. Higgins desperately reasserts himself over Eliza's "deserting" him.	Solo	Rhythm Tune

Scene 5: The Conservatory of Mrs. Higgins' House. Later that day.

21. "Without You" (see page   Solo   Rhythm Tune
142)—*Eliza.* [Tag: "I Did It!"—
Higgins] Galatea overthrows
Pygmalion. "Lady" into woman.

Scene 6: Same as Act I, Scene 8. Immediately following.

22. "I've Grown Accustomed To   Solo   Ballad (also
Her Face" (see page 141)—   Special Material)
Higgins. Pygmalion protests his
defeat. Tyrant into man.

(Scene 7: Same as Act I, Scene 3. Immediately following.)
Half-page scene, underscored
("I Could Have Danced All
Night"). Eliza returns.
Curtain.

Lerner and Loewe hardly started forth, of course, with this finished result (though it turned out that **My Fair Lady** required extraordinarily little revision). During rehearsal and especially tryout, the in-progress run-down does much to guide the *routining* of the musical—the constant juggling and perfecting of the *rhythmic contrasts* among solos, small groups and large groups, ballads and rhythm tunes, different kinds of rhythm tunes, comedy numbers and dramatic numbers, and all the rewrites necessary to re-connect them—including new numbers in the first place. The routining is sometimes held flexible as long as practicable, even not set (or "frozen") until just before the New York opening.

In **My Fair Lady**'s run-down, note, not every scene had a song, and some scenes had more than one: true of all musicals. The four scenes (out of eighteen) without songs needed none. They are the shortest in the musical: the first three in Act I are no more than lead-ins to the biggest production numbers in the show; the fourth is the musical's coda lead-out, and is the shortest of all.

In principle, it is essential to musicalize as much and wherever possible. Trim down later. Before settling on the selected dozen or fifteen or twenty-five songs that will make up the particular score for a Broadway musical nowadays, easily fifty to more likely a hundred, in whole or in part, will be written. That even helps in finding the most contrasting songs to accentuate plot switches.

"Rules" for scores have been proposed, incidentally. One such prescribes, "A ballad may not follow a ballad, or a rhythm tune a rhythm tune." **My Fair Lady** has four ballad-style numbers in a row: "I Could Have Danced All Night," "The Ascot Gavotte," "On the Street Where You Live" and "The Embassy Waltz." All are so varied from each other, musically, romantically, comically and in the way they are populated—in short, dramatically—and so much happens between them, there is no chance they will cancel each other out. Rhythm tunes also follow each other, at three different points: the reprise of "With a Little Bit of Luck" by "Just You Wait!," "You Did It!" by the reprise of "Just You Wait!," and in fullest counter-action, "A Hymn to Him" by "Without You." Once again, dramatic diversity, intervening circumstances and differences in the rhythms themselves ensure contrast.

Similarly dubious are injunctions like: "Two songs may not follow directly on each other," or, "Do not open a scene with a song if the previous scene closes with one." One illustration from **Company** disposes of both of these at once. In the middle of Act I, a partial reprise of "Company" is answered immediately by "Have I Got a Girl for You?," followed immediately by "Someone Is Waiting"; end of scene. The next scene opens immediately with "Another Hundred People." In Stephen Sondheim's next musical, in fact, **Follies**, he capped such juxtapositions in a new version of the old-time grand finale: the "Loveland" sequence in which six complete numbers mounted without interruption one after another to the climax.

Every good musical makes its own rules that work for its needs. Every successfully broken rule creates a new rule, to be broken next. There is in fact no rule other than making a dramatic point with a song in the most vital and varied way that fits.

An equally important way that a score works is to *personify* the musical. Music most fully essentializes the "unique reality" of a show. The scores of **My Fair Lady** and **Company** sound like the worlds they make, true of every musical of individuality. The plots are crowned by the score.

In addition, a score works to *integrate* all parts of a musical. There is a set of powers out of music alone—establishing songs, reprises, segues, underscoring, and relief and comment songs—which weave the musical into one fabric. Accomplishing this depends completely on how much all the collaborators share every decision. At the bottom lies the question, what is the musical's *idiom*? The score, which makes the most immediate and the most lasting impact, rises precisely out of how all the characters speak and behave, and thus sing and dance, and how their scenes connect and build. What world, what class, what period, what mentality and singularity shall each and every character embody and develop; what musical manner for all this matter? Its essence and incarnation is the score, mainspring of a musical's vitality.

Size and Length

Broadway and Off Broadway are less important as conflicting commercial choices for musical writers than as measures of the size of their show. What capacity audience should share the event? Some musicals are for only 100 or 200 at a sitting, to share their lighter or intenser energies; like chamber music, they are chamber musicals. Other musicals require 1,000 and more spectators, to absorb their larger thrust of energy. There are only a very few musicals, all exceptions, which started Off Broadway and then proved themselves when moved "uptown."

This is not a question of production size. Broadway small cast shows as varied as **I Do! I Do!, She Loves Me!, The Apple Tree, A Funny Thing Happened On the Way To the Forum, No Strings, Grease** and **Company** have energy outputs geared for a large auditorium. On the other hand, both large and small cast Off Broadway musicals as different as **The Fantasticks, Little Mary Sunshine, Your Own Thing, You're a Good Man, Charlie Brown, Dames at Sea** and **Boy Meets Boy** depend for their effect upon an intimate house. In front of 1,000 or more—**The Fantasticks** in a summer musical tent theater, for instance—the effect is distorted or destroyed.

One or two of the above may be borderline, but hundreds of now unnameable musicals fooled themselves in large part by aiming at the wrong size audience. Big energy shows have been cramped by little budgets or large fears into small quarters, while *chamber musicals* have been inflated by over-production or egomania. Some underlying assumptions—made automatically, no longer valid— might be at fault. One such assumption is that budget is the decisive factor in going on Broadway or Off. Others are that Off Broadway is the "farm" that prepares one for Broadway, or that it allows more artistic freedom than Broadway.

First, today's Off Broadway musical budgets of almost $100,000 have proven as hard to raise as the excesses over $1,000,000 almost all Broadway musicals now require. The pressure to pay off is as overpowering both places. Second, Broadway is the arena most in want of true new talent. The supply can never meet the demand. Of course the risks are higher, but so are the standards. Dependent on producing over 90% *new* plays on a trial-and-error, deadline basis, the Broadway theater has long been the most experimental theater in the world.

There are three newer options. Off Off Broadway is a fresh, live outlet, more open, less demanding, much less expensive, and the smallest in seating capacity and pay-off pressure. The trouble is, it has yet to develop a reliable existence on behalf of new musicals, and there remains the question of the musical's intrinsic size. The second option derives from the present drastic shrinking of New York theater business. To meet it, *middle-income* or *middle-size* theaters with seating capacities mid-way between Broadway and Off Broadway, 500 to 600, have been installed. Located for the most part in the Broadway vicinity, they have middle budgets and prices, with investment returns to match. Offering a middle-size audience for musicals of middle-size balances, this too can mislead. A show such as **Show Me Where the Good Times Are**, an adaptation of Molière's **The Imaginary Invalid**, which was conceived by the writers as an Off Broadway-size musical, was mortally damaged by being moved for a producer's merchandising ambitions to a middle-income theater, too big for the intimacy for which it was conceived.

A third option is the development of repertory or regional theaters into tryout houses. It was of crucial benefit, for instance, in bringing **Raisin** to New York. Turning to these theaters is so recent an occurrence, however, with so many local factors to be shaken out, that their utility, while desirable, is still unpredictable.

In all choices among Broadway, Off Broadway or elsewhere, writers need to fortify themselves against merchandising considerations, exaggerated hopes or artistic anxieties; they are all distractions. Estimating the size of the audience that best fits the musical's energy level is the vital measurement. Granted, such decisions are made somewhat thoughtlessly at the start of creating a musical. Once the *size* of the musical has clearly established itself, however, the decision should be set, then guarded fiercely.

The "underpopulated" musical is an incidental aspect of size. It now comes in three varieties. There is the all-principal, or no-chorus, musical, from **I Do! I Do!** and **No Strings** to **Your Own**

Thing and **Dames at Sea.** Its obverse is the all-chorus, or no-principals, musical. This is the *youth* or *group* musical, consciously or unconsciously "pop" or amateur in aim or tone and recently very successful, from **Hair** to **Godspell.** It has leading characters of sorts, for the absence of any principals would expose them as basically revues or dramatized concerts. But the distribution of parts is "democratic," everyone gets an equal turn. In different performances cast members may even exchange parts, making it not matter who plays what, a method begun by **Hair.** In between lie musicals like **Company, Grease** and **A Chorus Line,** in which principals are chorus too, a newly successful form.

The *length* of a musical is the next question of refining. Today's musical theater allows more diversity of length, from full to short musicals. A musical may start out in either direction and switch along the way, if its development so dictates. **The Apple Tree** was a Broadway show consisting of three one-act musicals; double and triple bills are acceptable now. The revival of **No, No Nanette** recalled the three-act musical, another possible form. Most interesting, however, has been the development of musicals like **Man of La Mancha, Your Own Thing, 1776, Follies** and the seventies' **Candide** which play with no intermission—*full length one-acts.* Audiences prove flexible about accepting shows shorter or longer than they used to be—as long as the time passed holds. From its Latin roots, "to entertain" means "to hold between," the determinant of the length and interest of any show.

Like everything else, how long or short is a personal artistic gamble of the writers. For a combined bill, some questions are: What kinds of short material mix? Should ways be employed to unify them, by the writing, the casting, the production approach, or should they not? In the case of longer musicals without an intermission, there are other questions: Does the "Kaufman curve" come out better with no intermission, for instance, or does it come out worse? What, in fact, are the purposes of an intermission? They relieve extended laughter, release tension or build suspense; they serve audience transactions, from business to social to sexual; or they simply obey habit. In what ways does an intermission hurt or help a musical today?

Fixing the length of a particular musical, thus, may also be reserved until its scope becomes definite, especially a musical first envisioned as short. To hold it down by prescription may stunt it. Whatever the idea, discover all its suggestions, develop every facet that fits. Much later, cut, mold proportions, adjust length. Get it, then edit.

Title

Literal or metaphorical, the name of the musical is its subject. Later the title tells the audience something, but first it tells the writers. It incorporates the musical's style as well, the way it comes alive. "Annie Oakley" seems a duller show than **Annie Get Your Gun**, "The Mission on Broadway" than **Guys and Dolls**, "Down East" than **Carousel**, "Tevye's Daughters" than **Fiddler on the Roof. My Fair Lady** and **The Most Happy Fella** are both metaphorical titles for central characters in the same kind of love story, but the shows are worlds apart, and the titles say so. Try some titles of musicals all set in New York, and the same holds—common subject, but an utterly different signal: **On the Town/Wonderful Town; Bells Are Ringing/How to Succeed in Business Without Really Trying; Funny Girl/Hello, Dolly!; I Do! I Do!/Promises, Promises; Pal Joey/Sweet Charity; Street Scene/Company.**

Contrary to songwriting, where the subject in a title is obligatory to start, there is time for the show title to emerge. Its name may arrive as soon as the *seed*. But it may stay elusive till the last. It may also become clear along the way, gradually or all of a sudden—a *title song* turns up, or a character or situation turns pivotal, or a piece of dialogue prompts it. It may turn out to be explicit or allusive, plain or catchy, short or—these days—long. The show title is a refining aid because it is a final check on exactly what the musical is about and how to say so.

Thereafter the title is the producer's business, not the writers', a matter of merchandising, not identifying. Said a Broadway theater manager, "A good title is the title of any hit show."

Point

Point—or *theme, message, purpose, meaning*—has been saved until last in this section because it is controversial and confusing. What is a *point* anyway, and is it necessary? The best shows with points work in spite of them, from the so-called *thesis* plays of Molière and Ibsen and Shaw to musicals like **The Threepenny Opera** and **Cabaret** and **Raisin**. No point is ever as persuasive or lasting as a good story—or only because of it.

First, *point* is not *point of view*. A point of view is mandatory, but a point is optional. Nor is point *attitude*, what underlies the spirit of the show. Second, a point is exceedingly difficult to keep organic, unimposed. It has a compulsion to make pronouncements, interrupting and stopping the action, making a show heavy and lame when it ought to be progressing and soaring. Nor should a point be mistaken for a *seed*. Seeds generate, but points, strangely, do not; they are ends, not means.

A point may be made, none the less, if it can be made to work. Is it concrete and specific? Does it make a *dramatic* difference? Is it an aspect of character? Does it heighten situation? May it be made a seed? If so, follow it through, as far as it can go. If it is a good one, it will make more point than expected. Only dramatize it, do not declare it—the aim of every tool in this book.

Stagecraft

There is a grammar of the stage which makes writing for the theater easier. To begin, the stage is divided into areas:

```
                      ── Cyc ──
                 ╱                    ╲
   Wings      ╱        UPSTAGE          ╲      Wings
  ─────    ╱                              ╲   ─────
    3                                           3

                          C
                          E
  ─────                   N                    ─────
           STAGE          T      STAGE
    2      RIGHT          E      LEFT            2
                          R

  ─────                                        ─────

   1 ────────  DOWNSTAGE  ─────── 1
```

Curtain Line

Stage Right and *Stage Left* are always from the actor's reference point, as he faces the audience. *Downstage* is toward the audience, *Upstage* is away from the audience. Other chief designations would be *Down Center* and *Up Center*, *Down Right* and *Down Left*, the two downstage corners of the stage, and *Up Right* and *Up Left*, the two upstage corners. All of these have shorthand abbreviations: SR, SL, DS, US, DC, UC, DR, DL, UR, UL.

The *Cyc* is the cyclorama. It is usually a large, curved curtain upon which may be thrown lighting effects or projections (of sky, sea, landscapes or more specific locations), and sometimes it may be painted, if it remains permanent throughout the show. Further, it screens off the *backstage* areas.

There can of course be more than the three *wings* on each side of the stage if the stage floor is deep enough, and the musical needs more wings. They are counted from downstage to upstage, and are marked off by high, narrow curtains, called *legs*, or sometimes by shaped and painted stage flats; if the latter are joined at the top across the width of the stage, they are called *portals*. They mask the *offstage* areas, but permit wide passage to the stage, especially for group entrances and exits.

Downstage and *upstage* are probably all the staging references writers may need to call upon, if those. All the others, and details within them, are filled in by actors, directors, choreographers, designers and stage managers in the course of production. Writers may include in the script whatever helps them visualize it, but it may be left to the experts in staging to execute and enhance what the script suggests, with accurate markings. If it is important, for instance, to indicate that one character enters from one side of the stage as another exits on the opposite side, it is sharper to say it that way than *enter SR* and *exit SL*.

In the wings means ready to come onstage. Doing a scene or a number *in one* means working in the downstage or wing one area all across the stage. *In one* scenes, a term carried over from vaudeville, are still an earmark of musicals. In most musicals in the past, a *backdrop* (or *drop curtain*) used to be drawn or lowered just behind the *in one* area to close it off, in order to make a scenery change behind it. When the drop is *in* (or *down*), this is also the *cross-over* area. Across it performers parade, chase, romp or whatever, to keep the action continuous, or to suggest time or place changes, even without a scenery shift behind it.

In one is still used for star turns, solo numbers, or special staging effects. But the *backdrop* has largely been eliminated in today's musicals. Scene writing, stage direction, choreography, design, lighting and stage mechanics have all grown so sophisticated and ingenious that *cross-over* scenes to fill in *stage waits* for scenery shifts have generally disappeared; when they occur now, they look old-fashioned. Instead, performers are brought downstage and into spotlights for a number, or its last portion, while any scenery change swiftly proceeds behind it in the dark. As a result, writers have been greatly relieved today from *writing for scenery* (or costume) changes by having to make up scenes *in one*. Such scenes now are generally integral, warranted and usually more inventive.

Either curtains or lighting effects may open and close scenes and acts. Since swiftness is so integral to musicals, lighting's flexibility and effectiveness serve to open and close scenes most of the time now, while curtains are reserved for opening and closing the acts. There may sometimes be no curtains at all.

There is an entire art to stage lighting; the effects writers need refer to are few: *blackout* (extinguishing all lights suddenly), *fade out* (a gradual dimming) and *fade up* (or *fade in*). The last two are also termed *dim out* (or *dim down*) and *dim up* (sic). The blackout is an exclamation point, an emphatic stop. All the others are like dissolves. A writer may add "slow," "medium" or "fast" to them, as further dramatic coloring, but such indications are relative and better set in the course of production. An additional device is the *cross-fade*, in which the fade out on one area overlaps the fade up on another, from one part of the stage to the next.

In putting all of the musical on paper, including such stage technicalities, a number of professional typing procedures for musicals are employed. The easiest way to illustrate this is by the following four pages taken from the typescript of **Company**. They are from the mimeographed *Acting Version*—the form in which a musical is presented to prospective producers, and likewise goes into rehearsal. It is quite different from the hard or soft cover published editions, which follow upon a successful production. (In point of fact, these particular pages are from the final *prompt script*: each performance of the show is run from the prompt script, and so are understudy rehearsals; additional companies are cast and rehearsed from it, and so are cast replacements. The prompt script is the clean final revision, put together from all the rehearsal and tryout versions, complete and accurate in lines, lyrics, stage directions, all technical cues, prop plots and everything else which keeps the show in shape.)

The four sample pages—note: *not in sequence* but from different scenes—were selected to cover all the typing procedures employed. The value of following them even from the beginning is practical: they prick and remind theater writers to write orally and not literarily, visually and not abstractly, physically and immediately and not fictionally and narratively.

ACT   I

Scene 1

> ROBERT's apartment. As the lights
> come up slowly, there is a table
> around which stand five couples,
> each of the wives carrying a gift
> box gaily wrapped. JOANNE crosses
> center stage and places her present
> on a bench, followed by SUSAN.
> SUSAN smiles at JOANNE who tokenly
> smiles back and moves away. JOANNE
> puts a cigarette in her mouth, LARRY
> lights his lighter and holds it up
> which JOANNE chooses to ignore and
> lights her own cigarette.
>
> We hear footsteps in the distance,
> growing louder, and a key in the
> door. At this point the lights
> are turned out.

                    ALL
Shhhh!

>   (ROBERT enters. Glaring spot hits
>   his face. HE jumps)

                    ROBERT
            (Shielding his face)
What's this? What the hell is going on around here? Huh?
Who is it? Who is that?

                    ALL
            (Intoning)
Surprise.

                    ROBERT
My birthday. It's my birthday. Do you know you had me
scared to death? I was just about to run out of this place
like nobody's business. I was. I mean, I didn't know -- I
mean, what kind of friends would surprise you on your
thirty-fifth birthday?
            (Pause)
Mine. Then again, how many times do you get to be thirty-
five? Eleven?
            (Pause)
Okay, come on. Say it and get it over with. It's embar-
rassing. Quick. I can't stand it.

APRIL (Continued)
I thought it was a wonderful little city near New York. So
I came here. I'm very dumb.

ROBERT
You're not dumb, April.

APRIL
To me I am. Even the reason I stayed in New York was because
I just cannot get interested in myself -- I'm so boring.

ROBERT
I find you very interesting.

APRIL
Well, I'm just not. I used to think I was so odd. But my
roommate is the same way. He's also very dumb.

ROBERT
Oh, you never mentioned him. Is he -- your lover?

APRIL
Oh, no. We just share this great big apartment on West End
Avenue. We have our own rooms and everything. I'd show it
to you but we've never had company. He's the sweetest thing
actually. I think he likes the arrangement. I don't know
though -- we never discuss it. He was born in New York --
so nothing really interests him. I don't have anything
more to say.

ROBERT
What would you do if either of you ever got married?

APRIL
Get a bigger place, I guess.
        (SHE exits)

MARTA
        (Having observed the previous, sings)
AND THEY FIND EACH OTHER IN THE CROWDED STREETS AND THE
        GUARDED PARKS,
BY THE RUSTY FOUNTAINS AND THE DUSTY TREES WITH THE
        BATTERED BARKS
AND THEY WALK TOGETHER PAST THE POSTERED WALLS WITH
        THE CRUDE REMARKS
AND THEY MEET AT PARTIES THROUGH THE FRIENDS OF FRIENDS
        WHO THEY NEVER KNOW.
WILL YOU PICK ME UP OR DO I MEET YOU THERE OR SHALL
        WE LET IT GO?
DID YOU GET MY MESSAGE, 'CAUSE I LOOKED IN VAIN?
CAN WE SEE EACH OTHER TUESDAY IF IT DOESN'T RAIN?
LOOK, I'LL CALL YOU IN THE MORNING OR MY SERVICE
        WILL EXPLAIN ...

AND ANOTHER HUNDRED PEOPLE JUST GOT OFF OF THE TRAIN.

1-6-49

AMY (Continued)
AND BY MONDAY I'LL BE FLOATING
IN THE HUDSON WITH THE OTHER GARBAGE.

I'M NOT WELL,
SO I'M NOT GETTING MARRIED.
YOU'VE BEEN SWELL,
BUT I'M NOT GETTING MARRIED.
CLEAR THE HALL
'CAUSE I'M NOT GETTING MARRIED.
THANK YOU ALL
BUT I'M NOT GETTING MARRIED.
AND DON'T TELL PAUL,
BUT I'M NOT GETTING MARRIED TODAY.

GIRL
BLESS THIS BRIDE, TOTALLY INSANE,
SLIPPING DOWN THE DRAIN,
AND BLESS THIS DAY IN OUR HEARTS --
AS IT STARTS TO RAIN ...

PAUL	AMY
TODAY IS FOR AMY	GO, CAN'T YOU GO?
AMY --	LOOK YOU KNOW
I GIVE YOU	I ADORE YOU ALL
THE REST OF MY LIFE	BUT WHY? WATCH ME DIE.
TO CHERISH	LIKE ELIZA ON THE ICE.
AND TO KEEP	LOOK PERHAPS,
YOU --	I'LL COLLAPSE
TO HONOR YOU	IN THE APSE RIGHT
FOREVER,	BEFORE YOU ALL,
TODAY IS FOR	SO, TAKE BACK THE CAKE,
AMY,	BURN THE SHOES AND BOIL THE RICE.
MY HAPPILY	LOOK, I DIDN'T WANT TO HAVE TO TELL YOU,
SOON-TO-BE	BUT I MAY BE COMING DOWN WITH HEPATITIS
WIFE.	AND I THINK I'M GONNA FAINT,
	SO, IF YOU WANNA SEE ME FAINT,
	I'LL DO IT HAPPILY,
	BUT WOULDN'T IT BE FUNNIER
	TO GO AND WATCH A FUNERAL?
	SO THANK YOU FOR THE
	TWENTY-SEVEN DINNER PLATES AND
MY	THIRTY-SEVEN BUTTER KNIVES AND
ADORABLE	FORTY-SEVEN PAPER WEIGHTS AND
WIFE --	FIFTY-SEVEN CANDLE HOLDERS ...

	AMY	
ONE MORE THING		
	I AM NOT GETTING MARRIED	GIRL
		AMEN
SOFTLY SAID		
	BUT I'M NOT GETTING MARRIED	
		AMEN
WITH THIS RING		
	STILL I'M NOT GETTING MARRIED	
		AMEN

2-4-23

                    ROBERT
Very. Excellent. Amazingly good.

                    LARRY
          (Laughing)
Joanne, I love you when you're jealous. Kiss me.

                    JOANNE
I hated dinner. I hated the opera, and I hate it here. What
I need is more to drink -- and look at Bobby, how desper-
ately he needs another drink.

          (The WAITERS enter again)

Here they come again. SIR. DRINKS HERE. TWO MORE BOURBONS
AND A VODKA STINGER! Do you know that we are suddenly at an
age where we find ourselves too young for the old people
and too old for the young ones. We're nowhere. I think we
better drink to us. To us -- the generation gap.
          (SHE yells at the other WOMEN sit-
          ting in the club)
WE ARE THE GENERATION GAP!
          (To LARRY and ROBERT)
Are they staring at me? Let 'em stare -- let 'em, those
broads. What else have they got to do -- all dressed up with
no place to go.

                    LARRY
What time is it?

                    JOANNE
In real life? Will somebody get us another drink!

          (THEY are delivered just then)

Oh, you did. So aggressive.
          (To the other WOMEN)
STOP STARING!

          (Lights fade on the night club)

I'd like to propose a toast.

          HERE'S TO THE LADIES WHO LUNCH --
          EVERYBODY LAUGH.
          LOUNGING IN THEIR CAFTANS AND PLANNING A BRUNCH
          ON THEIR OWN BEHALF.
          OFF TO THE GYM,
          THEN TO A FITTING,
          CLAIMING THEY'RE FAT.
          AND LOOKING GRIM
          'CAUSE THEY'VE BEEN SITTING
          CHOOSING A HAT --
          DOES ANYONE STILL WEAR A HAT?
          I'LL DRINK TO THAT.

Note the spacing. The character's name is placed in the center of the page, capitalized for easier reading. The dialogue lines that follow are single-spaced below it. Between the dialogue lines a double space is taken.

Stage directions are indented from spoken lines, single-spaced again, and enclosed in parentheses. Any references to characters within them, by name or pronoun, are capitalized for quicker recognition. *Page 1-1-1* further indicates how *certain* stage directions, such as entrances, special bits of *business*, or technical cues, are double rather than single spaced.

Lyrics are set apart by capitalization and block spacing on the page, for immediate demarcation, as on *page 1-5-42. Page 1-6-49* is included to show how lyrics involving more than one voice are set.

For numbering script pages, a special procedure is followed. The act and scene is indicated on every single page. Wherever the script may be opened—and whatever the scene in rehearsal—the page marks the place on the dot. It is especially helpful in organizing rehearsals by scene, song or dance number, a daily headache in company logistics. Every *new* scene begins on a *new* page.

After the act and scene designations, the page numbering itself is continuous, but only to the end of the act. Thereupon it starts all over again in the next act. **Company** has 6 scenes and 56 pages in Act I. After beginning on 1-1-1 (Act I, Scene 1, page 1), it will end on 1-6-56. Similarly, Act II begins on 2-1-1 and ends on 2-5-32. From one scene to another, the page marking might be 1-3-17, 1-4-18; or 2-2-5, 2-3-6.

In straight plays, the total pages per act, when typed as above (no songs, of course), provide a general index of the playing time. The rule of thumb is: one page, one minute; thus, a 30-page act may be estimated to play in the neighborhood of a half-hour. It takes experience, however, to gauge this accurately. In musicals, an estimate of timing is much less reliable. Songs and dances are beyond gauging from the page. The rule of thumb is: three minutes to a straight song. But there are many kinds of numbers besides straight songs, and experience is required even more so. A general idea of the relative length of the acts is the most that can be told. Though not a rule, second acts are customarily shorter.

A warning in regard to stage directions. Is too much dramatizing being turned into, or turned over to, stage directions? Is the dramatic action missing from the song or the dialogue because of this, are the *parenthetic* directions making the point? There are certainly important moments in shows for *stage business*—activities with or without objects *(props)*—to amplify or necessarily take over from the verbal. But no stage direction is necessary for what is already contained or implied in the verbal action. Only the stage direction *different* from the verbal action needs to be spelled out, or a *nonverbal* action without which the character's intention would be incomplete. In an eating scene, if a character says, "Have some cake," it is not necessary to add: "(HE passes HIM the cake)." Necessary, however, would be: "(HE hits HIM with the cake)."

Even if they help the writers visualize, final stage directions in the draft that goes into rehearsal are better limited to what is decisive. It is not a help to add acting suggestions like "sadly" or "gaily." Write the line that way. A Katherine Hepburn or a Bette Davis can express more on such lines with a gallant smile, or *vice versa* a veiled sob, than a writer can ever think of. Leave that to acting. The published editions of musicals and plays, full of all kinds of stage directions, are misleading on this point. They are emendations of the prompt script, with all the working solutions for the original production put into final form to guide all future productions, especially amateur, and the untrained reader. Writers sometimes choose literarily to enhance scene descriptions and stage directions in the published version, but that is extra, and comes later.

Finally, beware of *Greek messenger bits*, to coin a phrase. In the Greek tragedies, messengers arrived to bring on horrors more suggestively described than could be shown. As a rule, however, what happens onstage before an audience makes the impact, and what it hears about off counts little. Unless the "messenger" himself is so important, which will be rare, or the offstage event is essential but impossible to enact, make everything that is important happen first-hand in front of an audience's eyes.

Originals *vs.* Adaptations

Broadway producers and agents who come as guests to my workshop are sometimes surprised to learn that generally we have more originals in progress than adaptations. Many theater people regard successful properties from other mediums—books, plays and lately films—as "proven," and therefore better investments. Many also think them easier to remake as musicals. The truth of the matter is that adaptations are harder than originals.

The difficulties are twofold. The first is the hurdle, if not the pole vault, of translation. It is necessary to move *completely* from one medium with its conditions to another with very different conditions. Second, the spirit of the source material is what must be cleaved to, and the letter forsaken. The adaptation must turn into an original.

In both difficulties, the letter is the rub. It keeps backlashing. Bits and pieces may be lifted directly, but only if they lend themselves to the musical theater's unique energies and methods. To carry out the spirit of the original in the spirit of musical theater is the charge. Absorb the source, then—ideally—never go back to it.

Shakespeare in the musical theater is the quickest proof of the necessity to avoid the literal use of source material. Though many have been attempted, the *successful* Shakespeare musical adaptations have numbered only five, and every one by dint of wide departure. Incidentally, all of Shakespeare's plays but two (**Merry Wives of Windsor** and **Love's Labour's Lost**) are themselves adaptations.

The first musical adaptation, **The Boys from Syracuse** (from **The Comedy of Errors**), had only one Shakespeare line left, saved for a last-scene joke. The next three, **Kiss Me, Kate** (from **The Taming of the Shrew**), **West Side Story** (from **Romeo and Juliet**), and **Your Own Thing** (from **Twelfth Night**), were all transformations not merely into modern dress but into new frames of reference. The last, **Two Gentlemen of Verona** (though it might more aptly be called by its trade reference, **Two Gents**) kept some 400 lines (less than 20%) of the total of some 2300, and stayed the most recognizable in plot structure, but took the freest liberties with its details. The result conveyed more completely the original's larksome spirit than almost all straight productions do. Each of these, in sum, came to exist as a clearly new experience—the aim of an adaptation.

There are many stories about adaptations, more sad than glad. Each is unique yet typical. This one involves a popular play of the 1950's, later a success in film. It got as far as good notices in Boston. Yet it collapsed there. Its idea stemmed from freshly envisioning the naturalistic original in a highly theatricalized enlargement. Opening up and turning out its world and its characters had seemed both to deepen it and to make it new. But the "muscle" in this production, the director, had done the two previously successful naturalistic productions. As these now "changed" into something unfamiliar, he apparently took fright. He insisted on putting back more and more of the old straight play, in essence restoring the fourth wall, and throwing out more and more of what had turned it into a musical and expanded it. The production came apart at the seams. The letter had crushed the spirit.

Out of inexperience or ignorance, there is also an amateur kind of error into which adaptations may fall. A play does not turn into a musical by "spotting" places for songs and cutting dialogue to make room. That is not even a play-with-music.

Adaptations are too often bound by the sources they are adapted from. Originals are bound only by the writers' imaginations.

Industrials and Children's Musicals

These are each subjects for books, but they offer some helps which complete this chapter.

The *industrial* is a commercial in full-blown musical comedy form. At its height in the sixties, such as the spectacular General Motors automobile shows, it now appears in less lavish forms. Commissioned by corporations of many sizes to move their products or services, it is presented in hotel ballrooms, convention showrooms or on-the-plant theaters to private audiences made up of the corporation's sales corps, dealers or customers. Songs, dances and preferably a comedy book rather than just sketches are devised around a given subject, the *freight* of the show. Sex appeal and showmanship are primary. The energy must be overpowering: an industrial is sometimes presented at breakfast meetings to wake everybody up, and inspire them for the day, or the year.

Making the *freight* into a musical is the job. It is a good way of describing what is always the job. Here there are head starts. The subject is exactly targeted, the audience's interest is pre-connected. That does not lessen the intensive research on both subject and audience: the industrial has its difficulties, too. But comprehending limits and then filling them to the brim, around a center and to a specific end, are exemplary controls for guiding a musical.

Further, industrials lead in the use of *mixed media*. From the beginning, industrials employed *visual aids* to dramatize products or services, and pioneered in increasingly sophisticated still and animated projections, electronic devices, light shows and other technological elaborations. Mixing them together with live actors was the crowning development (popularized in World's Fairs), and musicals have still barely begun to take full advantage of mixed-media storytelling techniques. The first to exploit them was Off Broadway's **Your Own Thing** in the middle sixties. In the later sixties, **Hair** and **Coco** on Broadway incorporated some of them, to be followed by **The Me Nobody Knows, Pippin, Seesaw** and some of the *rock operas*, whose free forms adopt such techniques best. There is more to a musical than an industrial's technological superiority, but when appropriate, there is more of its technology from which to profit.

Children's musicals offer more lessons. Their subjects and audiences are as specific as the industrials', and require the same sharp focus and energy. They have no choice, moreover, but to concentrate on story, and to tell it as tautly and directly as possible. Its prime movers will be honesty, clarity and most of all imagination. The more imagination on the stage, the more imagination in the audience.

This is the cardinal principle to imitate: sustaining audience attention by increasing it. Children arrive at a theater excited with great expectations. When the musical is to be performed by other children, the interest increases. How much more must it satisfy when written to be performed by adults. To create, hold and advance the illusion governs all. Writers must believe and care themselves, no indulgences permitted. Children have not yet learned to tolerate things that are tame or unclear, or false or begged or patronizing: their attention breaks. They want to engage completely. In the theater above all, the Child is father of the Man.

Process Is All

There have been many steps in bookwriting covered above, with songwriting still to come. Bookwriting will still continue through the next steps. The emphasis on every collaborator keeping the book going never relaxes. Neither, in fact, does getting through to each other on every good idea, no matter whose, no matter where, for all it is worth.

All the steps can never be numbered. Talent ventures for itself, and work gives the most answers. There are more ways to go wrong than right, but there are more ways to go right than one. To keep the franchise, talent must take chances. If the chance works, the result is so much greater. If not, so much is learned. Either way, talent cannot lose; it is how powers grow. If the musical finally fails, it fails for the writers' reasons, not for that awful cost, somebody else's.

Above all, the heart of the process in musicals is collaboration. The record devastatingly bears this out. Since the American musical theater purportedly began in 1866 with **The Black Crook,** only six American writers have written *book* musicals completely by themselves *successfully*: George M. Cohan, Marc Blitzstein, Frank Loesser, Melvin Van Peebles; Rick Besoyan, Off-Broadway; and Al Carmines, off-Off-Broadway. Many more have tried, but only these six have succeeded; and five of these, Blitzstein excepted, are "Orson Welles types"—one-person theater machines. They not only wrote all of the musical, but were also producers, directors, conductors, or performers—in one, or more than one, combination or another.

For many reasons, collaboration has proven the way $99^{44}/_{100}\%$ of the time. The process is for the bookwriter to summon music, the composer to marshal drama, and the lyricist to fuse the two. The teamwork is as concentrated as it is in championship team sports: no matter how expert someone may be or how highly specialized his skills, each reaches his peak only in combination with everyone else.

How, then, to get collaborators? Ask around. Join workshops. The possibilities may be surprising. How thereafter to write a good musical? Write the musical you would like to see.

The Basic Elements of Show Music

Song Form
"Show Time"
Rhythm
The Voice

Moving on to music and lyrics does not leave bookwriting but simply shifts it into higher gear. The bookwriter stays as involved as the composer and lyricist were previously. Any composer or lyricist who is starting his foray into musicals and begins at this chapter, however, will not catch on, much less catch up.

It is admitted that separating music and lyrics from each other is even more arbitrary than separating the book from them. Music and lyrics apart are less than halves; together they make a sum greater than their parts. It is mere convenience to analyze them separately, in order to isolate the basic elements of each; to begin, those of show music.

The song, it has been stressed, is what the scene is about. If a scene is a main event, the song is its pivotal moment—the scene's scene. From basic elements to finished results, this is the main thing to try for.

Song Form

Both *pop songs* and *show songs* are popular music: *popular* here means the opposite of *classical,* "of the people," not of the elite. Popular or classical, the most elemental definition of a song is a main melody which periodically returns in a set verbal meter. True, there is a growing sophistication today in much popular music, but it stays popular not because it may be memorable but because it is rememberable. This goes back centuries, past the troubadours, past Homer. The language of the people is vernacular, easily spoken orally, easily received aurally, the most quickly assimilated and repeatable. Musically, it falls into a form most natural, called AABA:

A—The first statement of the melody.

A—The same statement repeated, to let the melody sink in, (be "learned").

B—A contrasting melody (the "release," "bridge" or "break").

A—The original melody repeated, to bring the song home.

AABA is a *natural* form, direct and unimposed, because it is how we commonly express ourselves under dramatic intensity. Receive a piece of news good or bad, and the reactions, with individual variations, fall substantially into:

How great!   Or: Oh, my God!
How great!   Oh, my God!
That's wonderful!   No, it can't be true!
How great!   Oh, my God!

AABA is the musical architecture of an archetypal human response.

It used to appear in neat sections of 8 measures each, the basic "32-bar song" that ruled Tin Pan Alley for years. Now the exceptions are the rule: the number of bars for each section is no longer strict, and sections within the song may not match exactly, either. The greater flexibility requires much stricter skills and judgment.

Pop examples:
"Sunny Side of the Street"   8-8-8-8: 32
The Beatles' "Yesterday"   7-7-8-7: 29
"Raindrops Keep Fallin' on My Head" 9-9-10-12: 40

Show examples:
"If I Loved You," **Carousel**
8-8-8-8, plus 4-bar extension: 36
"If Ever I Would Leave You," **Camelot**
16-16-8- 16: 56
"I'll Never Fall in Love Again," **Promises, Promises**
12-12-8-12: 44

The 12-bar melody, incidentally, is also a standard length of the blues.

The basic 32-bar AABA, when it is good, is still the most disciplined and pithy a song can be. Mastering it ensures that both composer and lyricist may go on to variations of the form with much more chance of success. Novice songwriters write around and around a song until they find this out. Variations of AABA, including variations of section lengths, start with slight changes in melody, rhythm or harmony in any section, labelled a *prime (')*, such as AA'BA" *(double prime)* to AABA'BA' (the chorus-and-a-half) and on to permutations of it that have made subjects for books.

The second basic song form is ABAC; it also has variations, and appears only a little less frequently. Pop examples are "White Christmas" and "Moon River." Show examples range from "Only Make Believe" and "Bill," **Show Boat**, "Embraceable You," **Girl Crazy**, "You're the Top," **Anything Goes**, "The Girl That I Marry," **Annie Get Your Gun**, "The Party's Over," **Bells Are Ringing**, to "Side by Side by Side" and "You Could Drive a Person Crazy," **Company**.

AABA or ABAC refers only to the song's *chorus* (or *refrain*), its main statement. This *is* the song. Sometimes it may have an *introductory verse*, in a pattern shorter than, melodically subordinate to, and always leading up to the chorus. This did not prevent a melodist like Jerome Kern, incidentally, from writing verses often superior to other composers' choruses. One of many examples is "You Are Love," **Show Boat**.

The third and last basic song form has a name with similar terms as those just used, but should not be confused with them. It is called *verse-chorus*, or AB. It consists of short verses regularly interrupted by a recurring short chorus, in two melodies contrasted to each other. The changing verse lyrics carry the forward motion, and outnumber the unchanging (or only slightly changing) chorus lyrics: the chorus must be recognized as such verbally as well as musically. Usually the A is the verse, B the chorus, of varying lengths ordinarily not exceeding 16 bars. Pop examples are most folk songs, "Greensleeves" or "The Blue-Tail Fly." Show examples are "Look to the Rainbow," **Finian's Rainbow** or "Sunrise, Sunset," **Fiddler on the Roof.** My Fair Lady's "With a Little Bit of Luck" is an AABA twist of it. In **Kiss Me, Kate,** Cole Porter used verse-chorus for "Brush Up Your Shakespeare," but topped that by combining verse-chorus with introductory verse and chorus in one song, "Where Is the Life That Late I Led?".

Two closing words concerning the *introductory* verse. It is currently little employed, in both pop and show songs. In shows, as it originally worked, the verse dramatized the question (or *situation*) the character faced. The chorus was the answer (or *action*). The verse, in other words, was a type of lead-in. Musicals have so tightened up in general that the verse has largely vanished, or decreased to a few bars to heighten the dialogue lead-in.

Otherwise, fully used, it may not necessarily come first, but arrive "in the middle," between two choruses of the song—the question "returning" to interrupt or reinforce the answer, like an extra wind-up. The verse of "Only Make Believe," in **Show Boat** as far back as 1927, came this way. More recently it appeared mid-way in the songs "Hello, Dolly!" and "Cabaret." It is not so rare in occurrence as one might think.

"Show Time"

Between a show song and a pop song, however, there is a basic difference. The former is a dramatic action, the latter is not. A show song is a heightened action springing from a dramatic context, and as a result reveals character, develops situation, forwards plot. It lands somewhere else from where it started, it makes a difference. A pop song has no such specific pressure and function. It is an entity to itself, which does not go anywhere. On the contrary, it is preferable if at the end the listener feels even more intensely where he was at the start; a pop song furthers moods, not actions, it would rather *wish*, not *do*.

Being music, a show song also serves mood, but as a by-product and never by intention. A mood ensues, willy-nilly. The more it becomes music to do something else by, the less a show song it is. It becomes a pop song only when it becomes a hit apart from the show; and a *standard* by staying a long-time hit. But these will be extras. It need only be added that the score of a successful musical phenomenally outsells any single hit song, including record-breaking singles.

The nearest a pop song approaches an action is when it carries a message ("The Times They Are A-Changin' "), tells a story ("Is That All There Is?"), or supplies a theme for films or TV shows ("Georgy Girl"). These are still self-contained, however, not situation-sprung or problem-developing, not full-fledged dramatic actions. And even as leanings toward actions, they are a jot of the pop catalogue.

To ensure its action, the show song takes special advantage of the AABA form. *Release* or *bridge* are words used interchangeably to define the B section, but for the writer of show songs the former is much more practical. If the song is building through the repeat of the first two A's, like water against a dam, it will *need* a release. The B will *break through* the rising pressure to unleash it, to become the song's turning point, and require the climax that returns the song to its final A. For dramatic purposes, turn the B into a release to build the action, ignoring that it turns into a bridge as a result.

In ABAC, there is no bridge, by definition. But the B is a rise right away, and the C another rise after the returning A. ABAC suggests a doubly-building action.

Both applications of song forms make a show song into a scene. A show tune throws a curve. It is the same rising curve that Kaufman called attention to in plotting. As well as a build, the song's climax may be a twist, a surprise, a reverse; it may be "soft" as well as big; it may start as usual halfway through at the release, or it may delay longer. But music and lyrics both go for a turning-point and a pay off.

By musical means alone, it may do so by lifts in dynamics; by rises in chromatics or intervals; by other jumps in melody or harmony, including cadence or key or mode modulations; especially by gradual or sudden rhythmic pushes, including tempo, time signature or accent changes; by combinations of these; or by extensions, tags or other resolutions. These technicalities are beyond the scope of this book. To climax songs, however, the composer-specialist needs to master all of them.

Show singers know one thing about big climaxes, cruelly so. Candidates descend on show auditions like locusts. Large numbers must be screened out fast. All are asked to sing "the last eight bars" of their songs. It eliminates the deficient instantly.

The built-in charge of show songs, their rising curve, is what engages an audience and lifts it. Some pop songs may be highly charged, but they do not build or go somewhere in the same way.

They are not *"show time"*! "There's No Business Like Show Business" is what all good show songs, the liveliest, the deepest or the gentlest, say.

Rhythm

The two basic song beats are *duple* and *triple,* or 2/4 and 3/4. All the other *time signatures,* from 4/4 to 5/4 to 6/8 to 12/8 and so on, are derived from them. A *time signature* is a way of getting the song written down. The vast majority of songs are 4/4, 3/4 and 2/4.

2/4, *up tempo,* is fast and lively. Based on 2 beats to the bar, it feels the most rhythmic because every other downbeat is an accent, and it will ordinarily have shorter musical phrases. It is a frequent show tune rhythm, rarer in pop tunes, because it has such a *show time* feeling. **My Fair Lady** and **Company** examples: "Why Can't the English?" and "Side by Side by Side."

3/4, *waltz time,* is a flowing, lilting rhythm. It has 3 beats to the measure, and depending on the kind of waltz, varying degrees of emphasis on the first or downbeat accent. **My Fair Lady** and **Company** examples: "The Embassy Waltz," "Show Me!" and "Someone Is Waiting."

4/4, or *common* time, is ordinarily slow and easy, an elongation of 2/4, based on 4 beats to the measure. The main accent is on the downbeat, with a secondary accent on the third beat, and fits longer melodic phrases most easily. It is the most frequent time signature of show and pop songs. **My Fair Lady** and **Company** examples: "Wouldn't It Be Loverly?" and "Being Alive."

A recommended exercise, even more for lyricists and bookwriters, is to count the beat (ignore the melody!) when listening to songs, till some mastery of time in music is gained. It will also furnish dramatic ideas—the point behind this discussion.

The waltz 3's, for instance, differ vastly. They can so vary their tempos, and the degree of stress on the downbeat, that they can range widely, from Strauss (the Viennese waltz) to Chopin (the "valse"); from "Falling In Love with Love," **The Boys from Syracuse,** and "The Girl that I Marry," **Annie Get Your Gun,** to "Oh, What a Beautiful Morning," **Oklahoma!,** and "Sunrise, Sunset," **Fiddler on the Roof;** from country ("On Top of Old Smoky") to gospel ("Walk Him Up the Stairs," **Purlie**) to the jazz waltz ("What the World Needs Now"); and from the farce comedy soft-shoe of "Brush Up Your Shakespeare," **Kiss Me, Kate**, to the comic-outrage tirade of the aforementioned "Show Me!." In anthem form, 3/4 finally includes "The Star-Spangled Banner" and "My Country, 'Tis of Thee." "Tomorrow Belongs to Me," **Cabaret**, is a 3/4 anthem.

6/8, by the way, may appear arithmetically to be twice as fast as 3/4—except that it has nothing to do with 3/4. Its pulse is duple rhythm, not triple: 2 triplets, with a slight accent on the first note of each triplet, or 2 beats to the bar. 6/8 was used more in the past. Gilbert and Sullivan employed it one way in patter songs, and John Philip Sousa employed it another way in marches. These are period sounds to us today. **Guys and Dolls** employed it purposely for "More I Cannot Wish You," for the great old-time, soft-shoe vaudevillian, Pat Rooney, Sr. Sometimes today a march still appears in a musical in 6/8 ("Seventy-Six Trombones," **The Music Man**), but more often it will be set in straight 2/4 ("Hey, Look Me Over," **Wildcat**, or "I'm a Brass Band," **Sweet Charity**).

The best illustration of the wide range of rhythms, however, is the translation of 4/4 into the Latin beats. Translations they are. Time values are highly exchangeable within the bar, while the accented beat may move all over the bar instead of staying only on the downbeat, including to the half- or *up-beat*. Latin rhythms comprise their own catalogue: rhumba, samba, mambo, conga, tango, bolero, beguine, bossa nova, paso doble, salsa, calypso. All are differently timed but highly accented, and all are much more strongly rhythmic than our primary definition of 4/4.

There may also be fast 4's. In jazz, moreover, different beats may be dragged, anticipated, skipped and recaptured in other displacements. In rock, a strong and equal stress throughout the whole bar may make every beat a downbeat, which produces a driving, overpowering rhythm; or the stress may be varied on other beats and half-beats in the bar, for still different effects. Vitality comes from accents, not speed.

Rhythmic variations are other technicalities which a composer must master. The moment he hears a musical idea, it is true, a composer would find it impossible to disconnect melody from rhythm from harmony. They are as inseparable in composing as character, action and situation are in dramatizing. Yet rhythm, like action, is the defining element that pulls everything together. Any melody set to a different rhythmic time signature turns into a different melody, without a single note change. Two of the most famous songs provide examples, "Ol' Man River" and "Over the Rainbow."

According to stories told by lyricist E. Y. "Yip" Harburg, the tune for "Ol Man River" first appeared as a rapid, tripping tinkle of notes in the original opening number *ice-breaker* of **Show Boat.** Meanwhile Jerome Kern and Oscar Hammerstein were looking for a "big" song to take advantage of the voice of Jules Bledsoe, the black bass-baritone star. Lyricist-bookwriter Buddy De Sylva, of De Sylva, Brown and Henderson (**Good News, Follow Through** and others), called Kern's attention to the ice-breaker, and suggested blowing up the tinkle.

In the case of "Over the Rainbow," for the film **The Wizard of Oz,** the first versions kept coming out symphonic and bravura, while composer Harold Arlen and lyricist Harburg were looking for a 10-year-old girl's "wishing" song. Harburg finally persuaded Arlen to turn the sound yearning and wistful. Both times, a rhythm change and no other produced the new songs.

In **The Music Man,** this is made into dramatic gain. Marian, the librarian, the small town heroine, sings "Goodnight, My Someone," in easy 3/4 waltz time, characteristic of her. Soon after, Harold Hill, the music man, sings "Seventy-Six Trombones," in a 6/8 march time, radically different but equally characteristic of him. But both times, it is the same notes, and scores major points. The audience learns more what each is like individually, a ripe dreaming girl, a headlong confidence man, while being led subliminally to a link between them.

Such rhythmic uses are a large part of dramatizing character *musically.* Rhythms were earlier noted as bases of character, and the extra rhythms character changes into are developments of character. If James Cagney is a "fast 2," so to speak, John Wayne a "slow 4," and Dinah Shore "waltz time," their other rhythms will issue from these. These other rhythms may even include such combinations or extensions as 5/4, 12/8 and so on, and more common today, shifts of time signatures between bars within sections and even phrases of a song.

It has already been noted, further, that Higgins and Eliza "trade" each other's rhythms in their songs, as do Billy and Julie in **Carousel.** So do many characters: Sky and Sarah in **Guys and Dolls,** Arthur, Guenevere and Lancelot in **Camelot,** Tevye and Golde in **Fiddler on the Roof,** and some of us tacitly in real life. Rhythm traces characters moving away from each other as well, and is another aspect of the power of songs to expand by compression.

Half the battle in both defining and advancing character may lie in the suggestions that time signatures may make. Moreover, situations or scenes have rhythms or time signatures, too. Show songs indeed are scenes. Professional show composers are those who hear the unwritten music of this best.

The Voice

The show composer must also, before everything, write for the voice; and the voice is different from every other musical instrument.

It has the least range of any instrument, but it has the most colors, as many as there are individuals. It has unique solo powers, and it may be combined in astonishing variety and effect with other voices and instruments. Yet it is alarming how young show composers will write melodies that only an instrument or even an orchestra can carry or write for the instrument they may compose on (piano, guitar, organ), and ignore the unique way the voice makes musical sound.

The voice must pause to breath, which requires musical and verbal phrases to rest and regroup by. It can go only so fast and so far on a breath. It must deliver vowels *and* consonants, make sense. It must also exploit the musical virtues peculiar to each language, and minimize the shortcomings. Nevertheless, more can be expressed with the human voice than with any other instrument: it is the most flexible of all.

There are four elementary registers. They are soprano, and an octave below, tenor; alto, and an octave below, bass. They normally fall in these *general* ranges:

Soprano:	Middle C to A below High C
Tenor:	C below Middle C to A above Middle C
Alto:	G below Middle C to C above Middle C
Bass:	G twice below Middle C to Middle C

(Lyric soprano is higher than soprano, mezzo soprano falls between soprano and alto. Contralto, the lowest female voice, normally ranges from E below Middle C to A above Middle C. Baritone, between tenor and bass, normally ranges from A twice below Middle C to E above Middle C. Lyric baritone falls between tenor and baritone.)

The normal professional range within any register is approximately 12 notes, an octave and a half. Few songs exceed that (except for trick voices), and in fact the majority of songs fall within a 10-note range. These limits are precisely what have produced the infinite variety within them.

Elemental as this description is, it is incomplete without including that the *timbre* or color of every voice is individual, and makes more differences. A dark voice in one register will sound lower than a bright voice in the same register. Indeed, individual registers differ infinitely in color and flavor from every other, and differ within themselves: light or heavy, warm or cool, smooth or rough, sweet or dry, "white" or vibrato—and mixed. These are the very pleasures in voices.

The 24 major and minor keys also enter. Some have different dramatic sounds to some ears, some simply appeal more to some composers, some may be selected as right for a particular song by a particular character in a particular situation. But something better happens in practice. After casting, the key is changed to the individual actor-singer's best sound, including the most appropriate sound for that voice under dramatic stress.

Principal actors are often not as good musicians as the ensemble singers, but they do not have to be; they may not even have as good voices, except that theirs are likely to be much more flavored. Composers should expect to write differently for a Carol Channing than for an Ethel Merman, or for a Rex Harrison than for a Joel Grey. They should even write differently when either a Julie Andrews or Mary Martin, closer in quality but still not the same, is the hypothetical choice. "Dream" casting, by the way, can be a most practical writing help. It may inspire songs to meet the power of stars. The images and sounds of specific people, stars or not, make things easier. This is not "copying;" on the contrary, it teaches the trade faster.

Much that is practical may therefore be anticipated in the writing stages, to be fulfilled in the production stages. No matter who is finally cast, key settings and many other adjustments are made for all principals, to take the most positive advantage of each one's best. The published sheet music of show songs, incidentally, is ordinarily different from the score version. It is usually reset around Middle C, for easier singing, and rarely appears in a key with more than three sharps or flats, for easier playing.

Clearly, the professional show composer should also know as much as possible about vocal technicalities. What keys, what harmonies will fit, for instance, vocal duets, trios, other ensemble numbers? The necessity will be to make decisions on the spot; there will be no time for meditation in the press of rehearsal and tryout. Nor may such dramatic choices be left at all to the show's arrangers. They are important aides, but the composer is in charge and the responsibility is his alone. Without sufficient superintendence, an arranger with the most faithful intentions cannot help but alter the song.

A last aspect of the voice is one of the musical theater's unique excitements. It is called *belting*, and it brings us back to *show time*. Easier to hear in the female voice than in the male, it is that percussive-and-brass sound that reverberates right through an audience, à la Merman, Garland, some of Streisand. The male belting sound par excellence was Al Jolson; today, Joel Grey as the "Emcee" in **Cabaret**.

Belting is sometimes regarded as a *second* voice, as if a singer had two (though there may be two distinct registers). But there is only one voice, properly produced with the same support all the time. The difference is *focus*: resonance in the head or in the chest (*head voice* and *chest voice*). No matter where the resonance, however, belting is a *way* of singing, an attack on a song. It is easier in the lower registers, and more recognizable to hear. But there is also high belting: Merman once again, or Mary Martin (or Flagstad, Sutherland, Caruso, Domingo), or a song like **Company**'s "Another Hundred People," or throughout Melba Moore's range in **Purlie**'s "I Got Love." (The last is an outstanding case of a song written to take advantage of a particular voice. Some voices, like Moore's and Streisand's, are freaks of nature, extending well beyond two octaves.)

More important than its exciting quality, however, is that belting may also express a major aspect of character. The sound suggests aggressiveness, "experience," as opposed to vulnerability, "innocence." Before Sky takes the Salvation Army sergeant, Sarah, on the date to Havana in **Guys and Dolls**, she sings in a pure, easy, high lyrical sound ("I'll Know"). But after, she sings in an upbeat, belted sound ("If I Were a Bell"). Another such switch is Sandy's, the heroine of **Grease**, when she finally joins up with the high school "Pink Ladies." These shifts occur in many musicals, expressing character developments each time. So do the reverse switches, when a belter going lyrical may express even more tenderness.

More and more, there are gradations back and forth, but Little Mary Sunshine or Bloody Mary is how it starts.

The voice as a subject for show songwriters will not be complete until matters of vocabulary, meter and phonetics, subjects in the chapters to come on lyrics, are added. Everything so far, however, reflects one striking feature. The musical essence of the human voice is a paradox. Within its narrow limits, it has the widest possibilities.

The Implements of Show Music

**The Lead Sheet
Ballad, Rhythm and Special Material
I Am, I Want and New Songs
Sum: Music Characterizes, Too**

In once again moving from founding to building tools, the lead
sheet is indispensable. Without a mastery of it, no composer can
successfully communicate his technical needs wherever they may
arise. This communication, starting on paper, requires constant
elaboration by both musical and verbal demonstration. It is itself
the result of all the composer's prior input with his collaborators.

Division of the songs into ballad, rhythm and special material is
the traditional way of categorizing them. It has several uses, and
especially helps the *routining* of the show by sharpening the definition and contrast of each moment of it. But a new means of defining
show songs may be more pragmatic. By concentrating on what
originates them, their kinds of action in the first place, they become
better realized in the traditional categories while leaping in character sharpness.

Again it will be evident how each collaborator is ever more dependent on the involvement of the others. So allied, the decisive
power of music to characterize is even more productive.

The Lead Sheet

The *lead sheet* gets the song on paper. It is a complete words-and-music skeleton which suggests every sound the audience will finally hear from the stage and the orchestra pit. Its requisites are exact and elemental:

1. *The melody,* with the time signature and the key signature clearly indicated.
2. *The harmony,* with all the chords to match the melodic changes marked in musical symbols directly over the appropriate places.*
3. *The lyrics,* with each syllable clearly spaced directly under the note on which it is sung.**
4. A brief *description* of flavor, style or tempo, added in the upper left-hand corner above the staff.***

From the lead sheets, songs are learned, piano-part rehearsals run and all the arrangements and orchestrations eventually realized.

It is obvious that a melody arrives in a rhythmic order, but composers simultaneously hear its harmonies. In shows, transcribing the harmonies is not only a musical question but also a theatrical one. Musically, harmony is *color*. Dramatically, it is *situation*. It completes the sound, and compacts the circumstances; it incorporates period and locale, and pressure and development. Without a single melodic or rhythmic change (though possibly tempo changes), "My Country, 'Tis of Thee," set to harmonies for Alfred Hitchcock suspense or for Marx Brothers farce, becomes two different songs. When music is sometimes used not as impetus but as contrast to the words ("Falling In Love with Love," **The Boys from Syracuse,** "People Will Say We're in Love," **Oklahoma!**), harmony is similarly decisive.

A melody is unfinished without these harmonic chord notations,

---

*When the bass clef is written out, with or without lyrics, the lead sheet becomes a *piano part.*

**If the musical notation follows its own spacing, and the lyric transcription its own, without matching up, syllable to note, reading the song is a mess.

***Any language that expresses it best may be used, Italian, American, jive: "Freely, brightly, moderately (moderately slow, moderately fast), with a beat, with a light beat, gospel-style, medium rock, blues rock, driving, strutting, tender, kicky, funky," and so on.

and so is a lead sheet. This does not require the composer to be an orchestrator, a speciality demanding its own expertness. Anywhere that the harmonic indications are incomplete, however, the best orchestrator with the best intentions cannot avoid writing a different song.

No matter who delivers it, the conductor, the arrangers, the cast or the orchestra, every single note of the musical's ultimate sound is under the composer's command. And every single note will have been suggested and authorized by the competence and direction furnished by the composer's lead sheets.

Ballad, Rhythm and Special Material

Show songs are classified under three conventional labels: *ballad, rhythm* and *special material.* Audiences expect to hear and actors expect to perform each of these three kinds of songs, and writers are expected to be able to write them.

Ballads go to the heart. Their ruling subject is love—wanting love, resisting love, winning love, losing love, amen to love. It is the most common, most needed song, and usually the most difficult to write; it has to be honest and unique each time. The distinctness of each one in **My Fair Lady** and **Company** demonstrates the point: "I Could Have Danced All Night," "On the Street Where You Live" and "I've Grown Accustomed to Her Face;" and "Sorry-Grateful," "Someone Is Waiting" and "Barcelona."

Ballads may have other subjects: pleasures, as in "Wouldn't It Be Lovely?", or sorrows, as in "Poor Baby." Further varieties include blues, torch songs, lullabies and spirituals. (Not included are the songs which use the word in a *narrative* meaning, such as "The Ballad of Frankie and Johnny," or "The Ballad of Rodger Young.") Ballads encompass, in short, all the feelings which are tender or soaring.

Rhythm tunes, also called *up-tunes* or *jump tunes,* go to the hands or feet, or the blood. Where melody dominated the ballad, rhythm now dominates. Rhythm tunes have no limit in their subjects or diversity. **My Fair Lady** and **Company** suffice again to illustrate how widely they may range. "With a Little Bit of Luck" is English music hall 2/4 time, "Just You Wait!" is 4/4 and really a march, "The Rain in Spain" is a mock tango in 4/4, and "Get Me To the Church on Time" is a fast but lilting 2/4. "You Could Drive a Person Crazy" is a mock rhythm-and-blues in a fast 4/4, "Another Hundred People" is a semi-rock 4/4, and "Side by Side by Side/ What Would We Do Without You?" is a parody vaudeville-nostalgia number, mixed between slam-bang and soft-shoe, in slow 2/4.

The old distinction between ballad as slow and easy and rhythm as fast and lively no longer holds true. In the above examples, there are fast ballads and slow rhythm tunes, such as "Without You" and "The Ladies Who Lunch." A more interesting question: are "Show Me!" and "Being Alive" ballads, rhythm tunes, or a combination, *rhythm ballads*? Whichever the classification, the way today is freer, and not a matter of tempo but of accent—how much stress, where and how often.

A song may fall outside either category, however. It is then *special material*. In nightclub acts, the material is tailored to a performer's individual quality or style. In musical theater, *special material* similarly exploits a performer's—or a writer's—musical or dramatic or comic strengths. Melody may dominate some (including coloratura or basso profundo stunts), rhythm others and harmony (in trios, quartets and so forth) still others. Overall, however, special material means comedy patter songs and big dramatic songs, or comment songs and diversion songs—either to establish, relieve or intensify the action, or as vehicles for virtuoso display. Variety shows (bills of unique "acts") are one place, after all, our musical theater came from.

Special material examples in **My Fair Lady** would include three of Higgins' patter songs, "Why Can't the English?," "I'm an Ordinary Man" and "A Hymn to Him" (WHY CAN'T A WOMAN . . . ?), plus some ensemble set-pieces as "Poor Professor Higgins," "The Ascot Gavotte," "The Embassy Waltz" and "You Did It!." From **Company**, special material would include the title song, "Company," "The Little Things You Do Together," "Getting Married Today" and the dance solo, "Tick-Tock."

Certain numbers previously classified might be designated as special material also. From **My Fair Lady**: "With a Little Bit of Luck," "The Rain in Spain," "Show Me!" and "Get Me To the Church on Time." From **Company**: "You Could Drive a Person Crazy," "Another Hundred People" and "Side by Side by Side." In fact, almost all the songs in **Company** were earlier called *cubist*, which makes them special material in another sense, to be dealt with in the next chapter.

Here are some famous pieces of special material. Though only a small sampling, they emphasize how free-wheeling the category is. The first half of the list is made up of star turns, the second half of outstanding writing moments, sometimes leading to memorable staging moments. (Each listing is in chronological order.)

Walter Huston: "September Song," **Knickerbocker Holiday**
Danny Kaye: "Tschaikowsky," **Lady in the Dark**
Ray Bolger: "Once In Love with Amy," **Where's Charley?**
David Wayne: "When I'm Not Near the Girl I Love,"
     Finian's Rainbow
Alfred Drake: "Gesticulate," **Kismet**
Gwen Verdon: "Whatever Lola Wants," **Damn Yankees**
Judy Holliday: "I'm Going Back (to the Bonjour Tristesse
     Brassiere Company)," **Bells Are Ringing**
Robert Preston: "Ya Got Trouble," **The Music Man**
Ethel Merman: "Rose's Turn," **Gypsy**
Barbra Streisand: "Don't Rain on My Parade," **Funny Girl**
Zero Mostel: "If I Were a Rich Man," **Fiddler on the Roof**
Melba Moore: "I Got Love," **Purlie**

"Ol' Man River," **Show Boat**
"The Buzzard Song," **Porgy and Bess**
"Zip," **Pal Joey**
"Soliloquy," **Carousel**
"The Begat," **Finian's Rainbow**
"There Is Nothing Like a Dame," **South Pacific**
"Adelaide's Lament," **Guys and Dolls**
"Rahadlakum," **Kismet**
"Steam Heat," "There Once Was a Man," **The Pajama Game**
"Glitter and Be Gay," **Candide**
"Rock Island," **The Music Man**
"Gee, Officer Krupke!", **West Side Story**
"Hello, Dolly!", **Hello, Dolly!**
"Sunrise, Sunset," **Fiddler on the Roof**

And to conclude:

"Too Darn Hot," "I Hate Men," "Where Is the Life That
     Late I Led?" and "Brush Up Your Shakespeare," all from
     Kiss Me, Kate; and
"There's No Business Like Show Business," **Annie Get Your
Gun**

I Am, I Want and New Songs

There is a more creative approach to writing show songs than the three conventional categories. I am indebted to director-choreographer Bob Fosse for this invention. He also sees three kinds of songs, but all in tool terms. All show songs are either *I Am* or *I Want* songs, otherwise they are *New* songs.

More practical than whether the song is ballad, rhythm or special, this method makes songs into scenes immediately. By concentrating on actions, it pinpoints the causes which produce the effects called ballad, rhythm and special material. Character and situation rule, from which will flow the action and style of the song.

The first two types, *I Am* and *I Want*, cover the great majority of show songs. Who and how I am, and what and how I want, or biology and ego, are the two elemental dramatic actions.

In the *I Am*, the character's *need* is to confront. It may assert itself in several ways: to define an attitude, to take a stand, to apply the past or to change the future. The action may question or affirm, yield or persist—but the character commits himself in some way. *To claim* or *to discover* some new or greater awareness is its essence. *I Am* also appears as "I was," "had," "did," "you are," "we could" and so on, plus their interrogatives ("What Kind of Fool Am I?", **Stop the World**; "Where Am I Going?," **Sweet Charity**; "Where Do I Go?," **Hair**). In **My Fair Lady**, there are seven *I Am* songs:

> "Why Can't the English?"
> "With a Little Bit of Luck"
> "I'm an Ordinary Man"
> "You Did It!"
> "Get Me To the Church on Time"
> "Without You"
> "I've Grown Accustomed To Her Face"

In the *I Want*, the character's *need* is to reach. It also takes several forms: to yearn, to crave, to pursue, to seize—to desire so strongly that, again, the character acts upon it in some way. The *I Want* has a greater innate thrust than the *I Am* to *turn character out*, to relate him more deeply or more quickly to others and to the world. *To strive for* or *to demand* something more or something different is its essence. *I Want* also comes out in other words: "I tried," "I won't," "can't we?" and so on. **My Fair Lady** has six *I Want* songs:

> "Wouldn't It Be Loverly?"
> "Just You Wait!"
> "I Could Have Danced All Night"
> "On the Street Where You Live"
> "Show Me!"
> "A Hymn to Him"

The variety both kinds of songs may embrace is limitless. If a song idea seems to be both *I Want* and *I Am*, ego and biology are after all aspects of each other—what I want often reveals what I am. In all cases, however, one or the other dominates. Deciding between them is what will suit the music to the action. For the music may make the *I Am* or the *I Want* action even more specific than the words.

The remaining five numbers of **My Fair Lady** are *New*. Each is written precisely to fill a need different from *I Am* or *I Want*. A unique—or new—action is behind each one. They are listed with their special purposes:

> "Street Entertainers," an establishing opening.
> "Poor Professor Higgins," a time-telescoping, enlarged segue.
> "The Rain in Spain," a time-telescoping climax, celebrating a victory.
> "The Ascot Gavotte," an establishing production number which segues.
> "The Embassy Waltz," the same, which develops to the climax of Act I.

New songs defy categorizing more precisely because they are designed to meet needs which are novel; this is also a large aspect of *special material*.

This approach should now be tested against four musicals chosen both for their success and their differences from each other: the two longest Broadway runs, the most popular Broadway "departure," and the longest-running Off Broadway musical. The songs of each are listed in order. The designations are based on what is taken to be the action in creating each song, not what actions they may have additionally served in the staging.

Fiddler on the Roof:

"Tradition"	I Am (We Are)
"Matchmaker, Matchmaker"	I Want (We Want)

"If I Were a Rich Man"	I Want
"Sabbath Prayer"	New (but also We Want)
"To Life"	I Am (We Are)
"Miracle of Miracles"	I Want (I Got)
"Tevye's Dream"	New (but also I Want)
"Sunrise, Sunset"	I Am (We Are, but also New)
"Now I Have Everything"	I Want(ed)
"Do You Love Me?"	I Want
"I Just Heard"	New
"Far from the Home I Love"	I Want
"Chavaleh"	I Am (We Were)
"Anatevka"	I Am (We Were)

5 *I Am*,   6 *I Want*,   3 *New*.

Hello, Dolly!:

"I Put My Hand In"	I Am
"It Takes a Woman"	I Want (We Want, but also They Are)
"Put On Your Sunday Clothes"	I Want (We Want)
"Ribbons Down My Back"	I Am (but also I Want)
"Motherhood"	New
"Dancing"	I Am (We Are)
"Before the Parade Passes By"	I Want
"Elegance"	I Am (We Are)
"Hello, Dolly!"	New (but also We Are)
"It Only Takes a Moment"	I Am (We Are)
"So Long Dearie"	I Want

5 *I Am*,   4 *I Want*,   2 *New*

Hair:

"Aquarius"	I Am (We Are)
"Donna"	I Want
"Hashish"	New
"Sodomy"	New
"Colored Spade"	I Am
"Manchester England"	I Am
"I'm Black"	I Am

"Ain't Got No"	I Want
"Air"	New
"Initials"	New
"I Got Life"	I Am
"Hair"	I Am (We Are)
"My Conviction"	I Am (but also I Want)
"Don't Put It Down"	New
"Frank Mills"	I Want
"Be-in"	New (but also We Are)
"Where Do I Go?"	I Want
"Black Boys/White Boys"	New (but also We Are)
"Easy to Be Hard"	I Want
"Walking in Space"	New (but also We Are)
"Abie Baby"	New
"Three-Five-Zero-Zero/ What a Piece of Work Is Man"	New
"Good Morning Starshine"	I Am (We Are)
"Let the Sunshine In"	I Want (We Want)

8 *I Am,*   6 *I Want,*   10 *New.*

The Fantasticks:

"Try to Remember"	I Am (We Were)
"Much More"	I Want
"Metaphor"	I Am (You Are, but also I Want and New)
"Never Say 'No'"	I Am (We Are)
"It Depends On What You Pay"	New
"Soon It's Gonna Rain"	I Am (We Are)
"The Rape Ballet"	New
"Happy Ending"	New
"This Plum Is Too Ripe"	I Am (We Are)
"I Can See It"	I Want
"Plant a Radish"	New (but also I Want)
"Round and Round"	I Want (but also New)
"They Were You"	I Am (We Are)

6 *I Am,*   3 *I Want,*   4 *New.*

There may of course be disagreements with particular designations. The total figures of each category would probably change little, however. These totals are enlightening and cautionary. In the above musicals, and all other successful musicals, the combination of *I Am* and *I Want* songs outnumber the *New*. If the majority of songs come out *New* in the creation of a musical, the writers are either innovative geniuses, or have not grasped how to write a musical at all.

Sum: Music Characterizes, Too

There are ways in which the composer holds greater power than any of his collaborators. His music either will take over the book and vitalize it, and brace the lyrics and lift them, or leave the whole thing flat. How he points, or counter-points, with music will be decisive. Musicals are still more often referred to by their composers than by any other of their authors. Moreover, by the rhythms and the accents of his tunes, the ups and downs and the builds and holds, the composer does a most particular thing. He is setting the *line readings*. Singing is still the most extended speaking we ever do.

Since music makes its own statement, it should express the action and reveal the character without words. Granted, it may be hard to spell these out from the music before hearing the words, but after, the music should seem to express them explicitly. It especially helps if it "sounds like" the title in particular (see the lists above), like the action of the *I Am* or *I Want* in question, or like *New* when necessary. Male or female, young or old, single or several voices, the music should enhance such character elements however it can. (The music may even be required to make the dramatic point when the lyrics may not be totally successful.) Words and music should sound allied at the start, fulfilled at the end.

Contrasting them may also have special bite. In **The Boys from Syracuse**, the lyrics of "Falling In Love with Love" say that love is for fools, but the music says that love is forever. This throws another kind of curve. We accept the words at face value but the music tells us better: the complaint of the young wife who sings it is curable. The same irony rules again in the musical when the wife's younger sister falls in love with her brother-in-law's twin, and sings

"This Can't Be Love." In **West Side Story**, a different tension is attained between the words of "America" and the Latin beat to which they are put. Catching how the young Puerto Rican girls who sing it are pulled between two worlds ignites the song. In **Camelot**, the contrast produces a delicious joke. The music of "The Simple Joys of Maidenhood" expresses a sweet young thing's fondest dream, while the words demand to be properly and violently carried off and died for. In all these cases, character is even more "beanstalk-sprung" and ripe for forward motion.

The ideal is that music make the most impact on its own behalf precisely while helping to hear the words better—as it were, its "vocalbulary." This is obvious for a love song. Yet what kind and how much of a melody does a lyric with a lot of jokes need? By a character with a lot of dash? ("Where Is the Life that Late I Led?," **Kiss Me, Kate**) With a lot of slap-dash? ("I'll Never Be Jealous Again," **The Pajama Game**) Several characters singing together, with the greater problem of making all the words come clear? ("There Is Nothing Like a Dame," **South Pacific**; "Gee, Officer Krupke!," **West Side Story**; "Big Spender," **Sweet Charity**; "Where Can You Take a Girl?", **Promises, Promises**) Singing and dancing very actively together? ("Magic to Do," **Pippin**; "I Hope I Get It," **A Chorus Line**)

Music to characterize by is the farthest thing from background or incidental music, *movie music*. It is foreground, not insurance for the point but the point itself. Nor is it *program music*. Songs are scenes, and musical description is exactly what to avoid. Nor is it *tone poem* music. A show song activates given moments, it does not report how they feel or paint their effects; *mood* has no action, though all actions have moods. Nor is it *art song* music. Art song's forms and idioms are classical; while popular music incorporates more classical elements today, a show song has to be a much tighter part of a whole than art songs can afford. The essential way to avoid all these traps is the same as in plotting. Resist telling an audience what to feel or think. Let it find out and choose sides, through character in action.

A show song is a close-up, sustained. Imparting enormous emphasis, it must count. As rhymes give words thread and point, melodies, by the cadences that compose them, and the portions and proportions that repeat them, also rhyme—to such physical effect that they make everyone in the audience feel musical, and to such dramatic effect that the song indeed makes the scene.

Additional Uses of Show Music

Establishing
Openings
The Reprise
The Segue
Underscoring
Relief and Comment

Before proceeding to show lyrics and filling in the verbal side of the musical matters so far discussed, this chapter intervenes. It must account for certain uses which emerge from and enlarge upon song's basic function of taking over and heightening action. This includes music without words, and affects lyric matters ahead as well.

All represent other kinds of scenes that songs make.

Establishing

Establishing numbers are the *I Am* song writ large. To "establish" or set situations is their action—in the time, the place and most of all the relationships out of which the musical stems, or to which it may need to shift.

All *opening numbers*, thus, must establish. They often do so deploying a large ensemble, in what are called *production numbers*, to get things started—not only plot, but interest and excitement. Many shows begin so; some rousers at random:

> The title song of **Company**
> "Walk Him Up the Stairs," **Purlie**
> "Willkommen," **Cabaret**
> "Magic To Do," **Pippin**
> "Fugue for Tin Horns," **Guys and Dolls**
> "Rock Island," **The Music Man** (the *a cappella* "railroad train" song)
> And indeed, "Another Op'nin', Another Show," **Kiss Me, Kate**

There is also an opposite kind of show beginning, the so-called "soft" opening. These are quiet, often (though not necessarily) solo introductions to the show. **Oklahoma!**'s "Oh, What a Beautiful Mornin' " was the pioneer soft opening that caught on, and an extreme one. The hero, Curly, was not even seen singing at first. As the lights came up on an empty stage depicting a classic American landscape of a prairie farm, only his voice offstage was heard. The soft opening appealed greatly to Rodgers and Hammerstein: only two of the nine musicals they wrote together had big-energy beginnings, **Carousel** and **Allegro**.

Some other examples demonstrate how widely soft openings may range:

> "Summertime," **Porgy and Bess** (even before **Oklahoma!**)
> "*Dites-Moi Pourquoi*," **South Pacific**
> "Try to Remember," **The Fantasticks**
> "I Wonder What the King Is Doing Tonight," **Camelot** (emerging out of dialogue)
> The tacit, choreographed boxing-gym opening of **Golden Boy**
> "Half as Big as Life," **Promises, Promises** (out of a quick soliloquy)

Sometimes an opening starts with a soft one and goes into a big one, as in **Two Gentlemen of Verona.**

Secondly, establishing numbers occur in a musical whenever there is a need to make strong, abrupt switches in the plot, like new chapters or new headlines. By definition, these cannot be "soft" but must be big numbers. (Though the word is generally used loosely, a *number* per se may be defined as a song that a composer builds up extensively, or that requires choreography to stage, or both.) The two examples in **My Fair Lady** are "The Ascot Gavotte" and "The Embassy Waltz," and the one in **Company,** though solo, is "Another Hundred People." A few notable others:

> The title song of **Oklahoma!** (with a four-line dialogue lead-in)
> "Hernando's Hideaway," **The Pajama Game**
> The reprise in quintet form of "Tonight," **West Side Story**
> "The Telephone Hour," **Bye Bye Birdie**
> "Big Spender" and "Rhythm of Life," **Sweet Charity**

Follies offers a striking case in point all its own. It seems to suggest the impossible, a score made up entirely of establishing set-pieces, in a parade of extended *I Am*'s setting characters up and setting them down. Each time the audience learns everything it needs to know, then the unbroken six-song climax, "Loveland," provides all there is left to know. **Follies** is a tribute to the establishing song.

Because establishing songs tend so strongly to become production numbers, they also tend to be *special material* or *New.* But they never work as short cuts or as padding, they work only because the action uniquely demands them.

Openings

There is more to say about opening numbers per se. Act I and Act II openings, in fact, present divergent questions.

The uses of Act I openings as *ice breakers* or *warm ups* are once upon a time now. TV's need to "grab" or "hook" does not apply, either. Today, more is at stake than merely establishing. Theater writers are hosts, ringmasters, conjurers. The style and reach of the entire musical rides on the Act I opening, as well as the subject and action. The audience is not in its seats but in the writers' hands. Openings usher audiences into complete worlds, and kindle high anticipation of the time to be spent there.

"Tradition," **Fiddler on the Roof**, "Comedy Tonight," **A Funny Thing Happened On the Way To the Forum**, or the title song of **The Sound of Music** are examples among others of how full, how different yet how precise such signals can be. For opening numbers can attempt too much. *Exposition* rears its ugly head, or stars are given a bigger or an earlier entrance to make or save the opening, or in turn demand a special entrance. In ensembles, whole groups, however attractively arrayed in costume and formation, are none the less strangers to the audience. If they come singing and dancing at the audience too hard, the words often get lost in the exertion. If heard, too much may be piled up, or worse, rushed through.

On the other hand, to open with dialogue, not song, may be even harder. More than courage, it takes skill. The energy level is in question. Does a musical feel like a musical till its first song? A dialogue opening must justify itself on grounds much more relevant than doing something "different."

Song, dance, dialogue or combination—to set up no more than needed and no less is the trick. Sometimes a "slow" start will reap rewards later. Sometimes a fast and furious start will kill the show off early. The first half-hour of **Camelot** makes the best overall opening I have ever seen—one single, thoroughly laid out segment. It starts in dialogue and continues seamlessly through three songs and dialogue, building "I Wonder What the King Is Doing Tonight" by Arthur and "The Simple Joys of Maidenhood" by Guenevere into "Camelot," first by Arthur, then joined by Guenevere. It is a superb model, and if the show could have kept mounting from it, **Camelot** might have been an all-time musical.

Solving openings is so difficult, in general, it often is a mistake for writers to begin at the beginning. It consumes time that could be much more fruitfully spent getting into the rest of the show. Even later, in rehearsal and tryout, the opening usually keeps undergoing the most revision. By discovering more and more about other parts of the musical first, better ideas may also turn up for the opening. Only after beginnings turn into agonies, however, are writers willing to accept this advice.

Act II openings are *re-openings*. They may be tougher than Act I openings. They are also more sophisticated today. They fall into two types, to coin headings for them: *advancing* and *branching*.

The advancing Act II opening might be described as a *lead-out number*, in not just a step but a spring forward. The Act II opening of **My Fair Lady**, in a flash of six spoken lines with music under, leaps right into "You Did It!." The "big test" of the Act I close had been left in suspension. It is immediately clear that Eliza passed it superbly but Higgins is taking all the credit—and the next situation is already under way. **My Fair Lady** retrieves its plot after the intermission by instantly progressing. The great majority of successful musicals follow this pattern. There are also "soft" versions of advancing re-openings, such as **Carousel**'s "This Was a Real Nice Clambake."

In contrast, the branching Act II opening is not directly linear. Its distinctive feature is that it takes time out for a special purpose: to gather up or spread out other, inner forces in the musical. Aspects which appearing elsewhere might be oblique or tangential, singularly fit this spot and augment the show's total effect. They are usually curtain up, no dialogue, number on. Some memorable examples of branching second act openings:

"Too Darn Hot," **Kiss Me Kate.** It takes the audience up an alley literally and figuratively. Set in a stage door alley, it branches out into more of the backstage setting that is the world of the musical. A jazzy song-and-dance number, it does nothing directly for the plot except to enlarge it with one of the show's liveliest textural moments, at the opportune time, the Act II re-opening.

"Steam Heat," **The Pajama Game.** It expands its particular factory world in the same way.

"Sadie, Sadie," **Funny Girl.** It does the same thing in a different way. It displays the leading character, Fanny Brice, in her clown role. She is seen in her public life, at work, against the plot emphasis on her private life.

"Take Back Your Mink," **Guys and Dolls.** It does the very same thing in an ensemble version, around the character of Miss Adelaide.

"Night of My Nights," **Kismet.** In a different key, it is a pageant that furnishes the most Arabian Night moment in a musical Arabian Night story.

"First Thing Monday Mornin'," **Purlie.** As sung by the men cotton pickers, it provides the musical's most potent Black South reality.

Lest the last two be counted mere extras, they put an audience very much in their debt. Both musicals would have far less dimension and texture without them. They are renewed demonstrations of a musical's power to say so much more than it is given credit for.

To close, there may be a kind of *non-opening opening* to Act II: no number at all, big or "soft," but simply a dialogue lead-out. The trouble is that it produces the same effect as an Act I dialogue opening, leaving the audience hanging. A very big number is likely to arrive to make up for it by the following scene, as happens with "Rhythm of Life" in **Sweet Charity** or "Grapes of Roth" in **Promises, Promises**. The result: *these* feel like the re-opening.

Sometimes, after all the wrestling with the problem, the Act II opening falls in when during the tryout the break for intermission is changed.

The Reprise

For dramatic usefulness, little surpasses the *reprise*. It *supplies* songs as scenes. The *reprise* is the return of a song later in the plot—but a return *to add*, not repeat. It succeeds by its thrift: it intensifies character acutely, advances plot enormously, and both in a flash. It is a prime case of "expansion by compression."

In the reprise, the lyrics may change to some degree or not at all, but two things hold: the title and the tune. The song must be recognized. It is this recognition that sparks the reprise's power. The music alone speaks volumes.

There is a fascinating exception that proves the rule, "Let Me Entertain You" in **Gypsy**. The title alone keeps the song recognizable through several reprises; musically it has radical rhythm changes, described earlier. Each alteration not only telescopes time-leaps but also develops the song into the musical's leitmotif. **Company**'s title song, with minor musical and lyric changes, is linked through various reprises to serve a similar end.

There are in the main three ways that reprises work dramatically. They may be taken by the same character. This happens to be how all the reprises work in **My Fair Lady**. When Doolittle returns to "With a Little Bit of Luck," he thinks Eliza has "moved in" with

Higgins: at last he can make good on his cut of the "main chance." When Eliza returns to "Just You Wait!," her metamorphosis has taken hold: this time its threat to Higgins is true. Freddy's recurrent adoration in "On the Street Where You Live" is all of a sudden put to the proof by Eliza's challenge, "Show Me!." And when Eliza's attempt to re-join "Wouldn't It Be Loverly?" is baffled, it confirms her intention to strike out for herself.

Reprises may also be taken by a different character or characters. This especially dramatizes the movement of characters toward each other, and often the ironies of such movements. Some prime examples: "So in Love" in **Kiss Me, Kate**, when Fred (Petruchio) confesses late to what Lilli (Kate) confessed early. "A Puzzlement" in **The King and I**, when in turn the young sons of Anna and the King, thrown together, face how to cope. "Tonight" in **West Side Story**, when everyone turns the song of Maria and Tony into a loaded fuse. "Hello, Dolly!," when Vandergelder, Dolly's long-fleeing quarry, is captured at last and and then leads the show's climax reprise. "I Don't Know How to Love Him" in **Jesus Christ Superstar**, when at the end, after the betrayal, Judas incorporates part of Mary Magdalene's song.

Another way that reprises work, alluded to in the reference to leitmotifs above, is by *linking* (to coin another term). A reprise may be linked to telescope time sequences, as in the use of "We Open in Venice" in **Kiss Me, Kate**; this is fairly standard. There may be thematic linking, as in "My Ship" in **Lady in the Dark**, which keeps appearing in fragments until the end of the show, when both Liza and the song come together. *Book-end* reprises may be another version, as in the use of "Try to Remember" to open and close **The Fantasticks; Cabaret, Brigadoon** and **South Pacific** also use the device. *Book-ending* must be used skillfully, however, lest it turn pat, instead of add up. Tunes may also be reprised in the underscoring, without the words, one of the most suggestive linkings of all, to be illustrated shortly in the section on underscoring.

The whole reprise catalogue can never be completed. Skill and daring are bound to invent other uses. There are, however, two limitations to be forewarned against. The first is classic. The simpler the reprise is employed, the better. The reprise accomplishes something vast and swift, which will be lost by complication. The other is the danger of over-use. It is very tempting to use a good song more than once, but that must not deflect writers from finding the exact song that fits. The reprise produces abrupt character development, and instant fusion of elements in flux. Its best effect is to perform an action a new song cannot.

The Segue

Two other ways music is used to carry through a musical are the *segue* and *underscoring*. Both involve music only, no lyrics.

The *segue* (SEG-way) is an orchestral figure of a given number of bars to *bridge* from one scenery shift to another, or sometimes from one plot moment to another. (*Segue* and *bridge* are used interchangeably.)

Musicals, always swift, have gotten swifter. The old way to bridge was the *cross-over* scene already described, *action bits* accompanied by music written *to segue*. Scene shifts today may be accomplished in blackouts fast enough to require only a brief *segue under* them. Even when done in full view as part of the show's entertainment, as in **I Do! I Do!**, **Sweet Charity**, **Follies** and many more, brief *segues under* still support them. (Interestingly, two all-time numbers grew out of the scene shift taking too long: "Hernando's Hideaway" in **The Pajama Game**, and no less than "There's No Business Like Show Business" in **Annie Get Your Gun**. This has gone further, more recently. Segues have become extended into complete songs out of exuberance, as in **Hair, Two Gentlemen of Verona** and a few others, accounting in part for the proliferation of songs in such musicals.)

The music of the segue stems from somewhere in the score, either literally or stylistically. Though an audience hears segues only subliminally, they aid storytelling sharply, as stings or stretches of sound. **Promises, Promises**, for instance, used stings expertly to cover passages of time. Choreographed morning, noon and evening ritualized comings and goings in the lobby of a New York office building also kept connecting and advancing plot development.

And therein is the secret. The segue is a lead-out. Films, with their instant cuts, can *tag* scenes with music, and often need to. In musicals, however, segues cannot do for the scene what the scene itself has not done. Segues function to anticipate the next event, to keep the story moving forward. Exceptions to this will be very rare. Telegraph ahead, just enough.

Some segues can be anticipated in the writing phase, on behalf of the overall vision of the musical and in preparation for technical needs. But the total execution, including continuing correction, of segues is subject to the show on its feet; no expert, no matter how seasoned, can foresee enough. Some can be accomplished during the rehearsal phase, but the process is finally dependent on the scenery, lighting and especially the costumes to arrive, when *writing for scenery* or *writing for costumes* again becomes imminent. Segues characteristically cover such *stage waits*, if they cannot be otherwise solved. On the other hand, directors and choreographers may want segues for certain staging ideas. Audiences may even require them, to guide and heighten their enjoyment. The segue writing will be finished only when the tryout is finished.

All the collaborators are concerned in decisions regarding segues—their style and their point. But it is the composer who writes them all—either by his own hand, or by the arranger-lieutenants strictly under his hand.

Underscoring

Expand the segue beyond bridging between scenes, and the result is *underscoring.* Indeed, underscoring may be the wellspring of the segue. Underscoring is the music that rises to abut spoken words, *under scenes as they run.*

Translate "under" to "within," and "scoring" to "adding points," and underscoring means to add points within the material. Contrary to background or incidental music, it heightens impact by sculpturing the action, putting it into relief. Ironically, it gains attention by making the spoken words heard better, it crystallizes the scene. In another mode, underscoring may lead an audience through a scene so that it cannot tell where dialogue ends and song begins: it spans the scene, specifying, as it were, the ESP in it.

Or it both crystallizes and spans. The "If I Loved You" scene in **Carousel** is one of the best examples of both uses together, and indeed a key to the musical's style. Musicals with other kinds of such felicitous underscoring include **South Pacific, The**

Threepenny Opera, The Music Man, The Most Happy Fella and **Two Gentlemen of Verona**, to name a few, while **Ain't Supposed To Die a Natural Death** made an odd but intriguing advance: the underscoring is tantamount to song. **A Chorus Line** made a unique advance: dance, carrying the show, is also turned into its underscoring.

Composing underscoring, whether in brief or long passages, also stems from the score, literally or stylistically. An existing song may be used without lyrics from beginning to end, but it is more likely that only a part of it will be used, of course re-orchestrated. The power of this kind of *reprise underscoring* comes directly from its economy of means. **Carousel** is again a classic example. Some of its underscoring was "new." But songs already planted accomplished the most. Not only "If I Loved You" but in fact one-half the score was reprised in the underscoring to make points: "The Carousel Waltz," "You're a Queer One," "Mister Snow," "June Is Bustin' Out All Over," "This Was a Real Nice Clambake" and "You'll Never Walk Alone." (This is apart from the sung reprises.) Small wonder an audience knows the songs when it leaves.

If segues demand effort, underscoring is a mammoth job. There have been musicals with more than a hundred underscoring cues; the conductor hardly puts his baton down. Like segues, much underscoring awaits rehearsals to set it up, and the tryout to get it right; but, much more than with segues, underscoring is planned in the writing phase. It finally takes consummate collaboration between the creative staff and performers and orchestra, to perfect the dramatic rhythms of each scene and the playing rhythms of individuals and groups. Fitting so many precision parts together is a victory and a wonder every time.

The last question about underscoring is the first. Every musical needs segues. Does it need underscoring? If so, how much? The answers can only be personal, and go back to the vision of the musical and its style.

Relief and Comment

These are the most advanced songs as scenes. They may appear to exceed or contradict the direct-action use of music stressed so far.

Relief songs may be divided into three categories: *respites, novelty numbers* and *interludes*. Comedy numbers, for instance, may seem *respites* that depart or even rest from the action. This is deceptive, however, especially as musicals have grown more story-centered. Where once the great clowns like Bert Lahr, Ed Wynn, Bobby Clark, Fanny Brice or Bea Lillie could interrupt a show to do a comedy turn, today the meaning of respite is *the relief of tension*. "Gee, Officer Krupke!" in **West Side Story** is certainly "comedy relief." But it occurs at a crucially fit place, to regroup energies, both the characters' and the audience's, for the big, final climax to come. In an interview in the *New York Times* (April 28, 1970), Stephen Sondheim, having moved from lyricist for **West Side Story** to composer-lyricist for **A Funny Thing Happened On the Way To the Forum**, put it another way: in **A Funny Thing**, "the songs were respites from the relentlessness of the comedy."

Other such kinds of respite songs that seem primarily intended for relief on the surface, but reinforce beneath as direct actions after all, range from "Where Is the Life that Late I Led?" and "Brush Up Your Shakespeare" in **Kiss Me, Kate**, to "You Gotta Have a Gimmick" in **Gypsy**, and "Motherhood" in **Hello, Dolly!**. Non-comedy respites range from such songs as "There's Nothin' So Bad for a Woman" (the "stonecutters" song) in **Carousel**, to "I Got Love" in **Purlie**. Most of these, it may be added, will also be special material or *New* songs.

Novelty numbers may be defined as providing an opposite kind of relief from *respite*. Where respite relaxes tension, a novelty number steps it up. It demands the most virtuosity or personality in writing or performance, and unashamedly calls attention to itself. Gilbert and Sullivan were its past masters. Classic novelty songs in today's musicals run from "Tschaikowsky" in **Lady in the Dark**, "Zip" in **Pal Joey**, and "Once in Love with Amy" in **Where's Charley?**, all the way to "When the Idle Poor" and "The Begat" in **Finian's Rainbow**, "Gesticulate" and "Rahadlakum" in **Kismet**, "There Once Was a Man" in **The Pajama Game**, "King Herod's Song" in **Jesus Christ Superstar**, and some of the *branching* Act II openings named earlier. Again, novelty numbers are usually special material or *New* songs, and are not restricted to comedy. An entire section, in fact, could be devoted to two shows alone, **Hair** for the innovations and **Follies** for the advances, each brought to the novelty number.

Some of the above numbers may not be exclusively *respite* or *novelty*, but overlap. The aim, however, is to distinguish the polar difference between them. In any event, each is ticklish to write. To what degree it may depart either from the plot or the style is one question, but whether the departure enhances or disrupts is the important question. Two musicals, the Marseilles-waterfront **Fanny** and the Amish-country **Plain and Fancy**, are not the only examples of shows which felt a need to "jazz themselves up" by novelty numbers (coincidentally in both cases, belly dances), and succeeded instead in puncturing the world each had ordained. Judgment is on the line as much as skill.

Third, and a poor last, comes the *interlude* song—to be avoided. Interludes are musical passages, two or three bars long, which in some songs fill in between sections of lyrics; some musicals attempt entire "interlude songs" to fill in between sections of action. More than marking time, however, they halt it; they relieve too much. Or they bog themselves in exposition, on the mistaken assumptions that narrating to music is dramatizing and announcements in lyrics are actions. They are misguided ways out of trouble, or betray misunderstanding of how show songs work in the first place; many musicals fail because their songs are mostly interludes. Since as far back as the forties, the only successful examples I can find are these five: "Moonshine Lullaby" in **Annie Get Your Gun**, "Poor Professor Higgins" in **My Fair Lady**, "Baby, Dream Your Dream" in **Sweet Charity**, "The Money Song" (I'M SITTING PRETTY) in **Cabaret**, and "I Just Heard" in **Fiddler on the Roof.**

It is no coincidence that all five happen to be songs expressing attitudes or taking issue; that may be the only way to make them count dramatically. And this "segues" into the unique kind of song savored for last, the most interesting and difficult of all: the *comment* song.

There are at least three types of comment songs. Its most obvious version is the song that interrupts the action to editorialize. Examples define it best: "You've Got To Be Taught" in **South Pacific**; "The Big Black Giant" in **Me and Juliet**; "Sodomy," "Air," "Initials," "Easy to Be Hard" and others in **Hair**; or "Momma, Look Sharp" in **1776.** To make this kind of song work, skill counts as supremely as sincerity.

Second are more integrated and evocative kinds of comment songs. These step outside the action precisely to amplify it; they provide another look that rearranges viewpoints, injects contrasts, adds levels. Examples include many of Kurt Weill's song grafts on Brecht's plays and his songs for **Johnny Johnson**, as well as songs in such varied plays-with-music as **Marat/Sade, 1776** and **Purlie.** Such attitude songs are also the stock in trade of the revue. The liveliest versions occur beyond the play-with-music and the revue, however. They are the ones intrinsic to the *integrated* musical. "Ol'

Man River," **Show Boat**, is an early example; others include "Summertime," **Porgy and Bess**, "Pirate Jenny," **The Threepenny Opera**, "America," **West Side Story**, and "Sunrise, Sunset," **Fiddler on the Roof**. *Branching* Act II openings are prime examples. The titles of such songs already indicate their comments. Perhaps they are all high intensifications of the *I Am* song, especially in forms expressing "we are," "you are," "he/she is" or "they are." Or the comments may all be implied, as in the score of **Grease**, a 1970's musical step-up from revue, a brilliant parody of rock 'n' roll, and the score of **Over Here!**, the Andrews Sisters "revival," a sharp satire of 1940's close harmony.

The fullest type of comment song, however, is exemplified in **Company**. After earlier starts in this direction, particularly in **Anyone Can Whistle**, Stephen Sondheim followed through such intentions so strongly in his **Company** score that its initial controversial effect may some day prove its attraction. Sondheim acknowledges in the *New York Times* interview previously cited that in **Company** "half of the songs come very unexpected." He called them "a combination—respites that are comments," and also "the subtext of the scenes." In addition, "One's interest in the score is in keeping everyone in the cast alive."

The comments emerge not alongside but within the story-line, and that is their accomplishment. Having termed **Company**'s songs *cubist* earlier, it is time to make the case. By *cubist* I mean that the songs display the central character, Robert, in multiple angles, stemming from the different viewpoints his friends have of him; throughout the musical, in fact, in a Picasso-like technique for the stage, Robert, as well as his world, are constantly fragmented and reassembled. By actual count, as will be specified in the run-down that follows, only four out of the total of fifteen are direct-action songs; the other eleven (eight out of ten ensemble numbers, and three out of five solos) are *cubist* either in themselves, or in the way they annex their comment. The four not *cubist* are starred (*).

Place: New York City. *Time:* Now.

Act I

Scene 1: Robert's Apartment.
1. "Company" (see page 123)—*Entire Company.*
    Ensemble   Special Material
Sung by the company: the five couples and three single girls who make up Robert's world. It presents a many-sided view of Robert, a "composite" of him by all his friends. Its action is outside the situation (the surprise birthday party), and at the same time amplifies it

in expectation of his arrival. It is a neat trick to open, for Robert will not even arrive at the close.

Scene 2: Sarah and Harry's Living Room.
2. "The Little Things You Do Together" (see page 146)—*Joanne and Four Couples.*
Ensemble   Rhythm Tune (also Special Material)
While Robert visits with Sarah and Harry (the "karate" couple), in the first particularized relationship, Joanne, the three-time married friend ('The Ladies Who Lunch"), leads the four other couples in a song accompanying and countering the scene. In fact, it is a tripled comment, on Robert, on Sarah and Harry, and on themselves—*cubism* overlaid.

3. "Sorry-Grateful" (see page 22)—*Harry, David, Larry.*
Male Trio   Ballad
An almost immediate answering male view of marriage, by three of Robert's husband-friends, a comment in contrast. It takes place as a *stop-action*, to let other actions in.**

(Scene 3: Peter and Susan's Terrace.)
A quick scene, no song, though some underscoring.

Scene 4: Jenny and David's Den.
4. "You Could Drive a Person Crazy" (see page 129)—*April, Kathy, Marta*
Female Trio   Rhythm Tune
More fragmentation, heightened by the syncopation, in a forties "Andrews Sisters" parody. Robert, center stage with Jenny and David (the "square" couple trying their first pot), is protesting he is ready for marriage any time. But at the side of the stage Robert's three girl friends present another view. Wailing the same tune, gathering together and snapping apart, they cut Robert up, in close harmony.

5. "Have I Got a Girl for You?" (WHADDY WANNA GET MARRIED FOR?)—*Husbands.*
Male Quintet   Rhythm Tune
Parts of "Company" have by now turned into the musical's "cubist leitmotif," in reprises or the underscoring. Suddenly it serves as a verse introduction to a song by all five husbands, sung in another stop-action. Full of male-bonding and sex-fantasizing, they turn their backs on their wives—and on "Sorry-Grateful," too.

**Stop-action is a name for abruptly suspending time, in order to add dramatic elements.*

*6. "Someone Is Waiting" (A SUSAN SORT OF SARAH,/A JEN-
NYISH JOANNE, . . . /SWEET AS CRAZY AMY. . .)—*Robert.*
Solo   Ballad

Robert's instant reply, no dialogue intervening. It is his first fum-
bling step toward commitment, and the first direct-action song in
the musical, from the single focus of Robert (though focused on
women in the plural).

Scene 5: Park Bench.
7. "Another Hundred People" (see page 132)—*Marta.*
Solo   Rhythm Tune

Instantly again, the answer-comment of Marta (the "kook-
intellectual" of the girl friends). The song then encores to
punctuate successive scenes of Robert with each of his three girls.
It issues not out of the action but as a "running moral" to it, like
earlier songs. The repetitions mount so ironically in relation to each
pairing, it takes the heart out of anything that could be specific
between any—and crystallizes the New York affect.

Scene 6: Amy's Kitchen.
*8. "Getting Married Today" (see page 70)—*Amy, Paul and
Company.*
Ensemble   Special Material

Amy panics on her wedding day, after having lived "all these years"
with Paul. The second direct-action song in the show (though it has
within it a counterpoint section, BLESS THIS DAY . . . THIS
GOLDEN DAY . . . THIS DREADFUL DAY. . . , which infiltrates
a comment).

Then another quick, ironic "Company" leitmotif, a flash to Robert's
apartment and the waiting party scene again, and Curtain.

ACT II

Scene 1: Robert's Apartment.
 9. "Side by Side by Side"/
10. "What Would We Do Without You?"—*Robert and Company.*
Ensemble   Production Number

Re-opening flash pick-up of the party, but *branching* into another
stop-action that erupts into the biggest production number of the
show. With straw hat and cane, and tongue in cheek, Robert and the
five couples toast friendship in two songs back-to-back, sung and
hoofed side-by-side, except that Robert has no one at his side. A

single man's friendship with couples is revealed as a vaudeville routine; the vaudeville doubles the bite, a comment on a comment.

Scene 2: Robert's Apartment.
11. "Poor Baby" (POOR BABY, /ALL ALONE . . . /WE'RE THE ONLY TENDERNESS/HE'S EVER KNOWN . . .)—*Wives.*
   Female Quintet   Ballad
All five wives, preparing for bed, share the same maternal fantasy about Robert's loneliness; Robert is preparing to bed April, the airline stewardess. Reality comments on fantasy.

12. "Tick-Tock"—*Kathy*
   Solo Dance   Special Material
In direct continuation, the third girl and the one who is least a "New Yorker," Kathy, dances against stings of dialogue the passage of love in the night: intimate acts *versus* private thoughts. The marrieds are in bed, too.

*13. "Barcelona" (see page 134)—*Robert and April.*
   Duet   Ballad
Robert and April awake, very early in the morning. The third direct-action song: she stays in bed. (Yet even here the song, as keyed by the title, makes extended outside references the very casualness of which startles.)

(Scene 3: Peter and Susan's Terrace.)
A very quick scene, no song.

Scene 4: A Private Nightclub.
14. "The Ladies Who Lunch" (see page 139)—*Joanne.*
   Solo   Rhythm Tune
Through all her sisters-under-the-skin Joanne comments on herself; a "multiple self-exposure" in a stop-action soliloquy of mocking protest against a woman's life of "hanging in."

*15. "Being Alive" (see page 136)—*Robert.*
   Solo   Ballad
The fourth direct-action song, and last of the musical: Robert adds up the score against the company of his friends. He is willing for commitment at last.

Instant, surprise birthday party scene back at the apartment (**Scene 5**)—without him. Curtain.

   This run-down of the songs of **Company** is the finished result. Once more, it hardly leaped full-armored like Athena from the

brow of Sondheim. As with every good score, the numbers themselves as well as their routing took enormous time, extensive
labor and unending collaboration.

A word about the manner of reprising. The title song keeps returning, leitmotif throughout. But the other reprises appear only as
mounting encores, within the scenes in which they first occur.
There are five in all: "The Little Things You Do Together,"
"Another Hundred People," Side by Side by Side," "Poor Baby"
and "Being Alive." With comment songs, the comment bears specifically on the moment and will rarely support reprising without
turning pat. In the *direct-action* songs, the action in each case is
good once only. In the case of "Being Alive," its encore is its completion.

It should be added that running certain songs in succession without interruption intensified their comments. Exceeding the standard ways that songs dramatize in musical theater, the entire score
of **Company** is advanced, seeking a new meaning for the term *special material.* Indeed, attempting only *New* songs is to be the direction much of Sondheim's subsequent work would take.

There may be other and future ways to write comment songs. In
Company, Sondheim succeeded by going back to a basic impulse of
drama and his own most personal impulse, irony. Certainly all good
show songs achieve an extra comment whenever their imme-
diacies are so essential they become universal, the natural aim
of writers—not to illustrate but to illuminate human nature. But
Company develops musical comedy into an orchestra of comments.
The result dramatizes how much at bottom we live self-observing,
ironic, cubist lives. This is also natural. For theater is the original
ironic, cubist place, actor and audience addressing and reflecting
each other. Musical theater—spinner of words, dance, acting and
song—is now its most alive storyteller.

The Basic Elements of Show Lyrics

Lyric Form
Vocabularies
Titles

Show lyricists are the most in demand on Broadway and the shortest in supply. Lyric writing is the hardest craft of all. It comes last in this book because it has all to do with adding up. The lyricist can least afford to slight the previous chapters: even more than the bookwriter, he is the collaborator who meshes the work of everyone else. His words make music make drama.

The words must rise out of the plot into crystal shapes. They must make music every time; the lyricist must be a musician by instinct, if not by training. Then, above all, in union with the music, the words must create *a thing done*, drama.

Lyric Form

Songs are still scenes, and words and music are halves that still make a greater whole. If the lyricist begins by setting words in, say, ABAC, the song form of the music will follow. In short, lyric form is also song form, and in practice they are mutually interactive, a joint product. To that end, the lyricist's clues to find the song are exactly the same as the composer's—to make his rhythmic sense explicit, of the character at the moment, of the action and its development.

The question of which comes first, words or music, intrigues many, but it is not material. The answer is practical, and individual. With Hart, Rodgers more often wrote the music before the words; with Hammerstein, more often after. Lerner once said that for the composer's sake in a rhythm tune he used to write out the complete lyric first; but for a ballad, only the first line, or agree on just the title. Bock and Harnick, and Kander and Ebb, work back and forth from the beginning. Working back and forth is unavoidable by the end, however. To complete the music by the words, or the words by the music, is all the job, and the joy.

An enormous amount of exchanging, exploring, demonstrating, testing, building ideas must go on *beforehand* between the lyricist and composer. Too soon to paper is the curse of many inexperienced collaborators. There is all the groundwork from *seed* to *style* to lay, as well as faith, hope and clarity between each other to establish. The best way is face to face, utterly open, and strong and trusting enough to say or try the dumb things that lead to the smart things.

In a show lyric, each word counts crucially, none may be wasted. It is one of the most compact pieces of exactness ever invented: the economy comes from selecting the essential. The stronger the form of the lyric, therefore, the more it can say, and the more music it can free; again, compression is expansion. Genius or inspiration or empathy may sometimes succeed in a flash. But the rule is hard labor. And there is no hope at all unless agreement is first found on the song's substance and shape; they are inseparable.

There are ways to write down words, when ready, which then can help decisively, there is such a thing as a *verbal* or *visual* lead sheet for lyrics. A published edition of "By the Time I Get to Phoenix" confoundingly looks like this:

BY THE TIME I GET TO PHOENIX SHE'LL BE RISIN',
SHE'LL FIND THE NOTE I LEFT HANGIN' ON HER DOOR.

SHE'LL LAUGH WHEN SHE READS THE PART THAT SAYS
I'M LEAVIN', 'CAUSE I'VE LEFT THAT GIRL
SO MANY TIMES BEFORE. BY THE TIME
I MAKE ALBUQUERQUE SHE'LL BE WORKIN'.
SHE'LL PROB'LY STOP AT LUNCH AND GIVE ME A CALL.
BUT, SHE'LL JUST HEAR THAT PHONE KEEP ON RINGIN'
OFF THE WALL, THAT'S ALL. BY THE TIME
I MAKE OKLAHOMA SHE'LL BE SLEEPIN'.
SHE'LL TURN SOFTLY AND CALL MY NAME OUT LOW.
AND SHE'LL CRY JUST TO THINK I'D REALLY LEAVE HER,
'THO' TIME AND TIME I'VE TRIED TO TELL HER SO,
SHE JUST DIDN'T KNOW, I WOULD REALLY GO.

Jimmy Webb, as his own composer, and further as his own performer, perhaps felt no need to write his lyric to himself in the clearest form. But that is precisely what the lyricist needs to do for his composer-collaborator. The tune of "Phoenix" certainly comes out differently from the suggestions the words in the above order make. Organized visually to reflect the actual song form taken, the lyric can be verbally reproduced in a form much easier for a composer to apply, or more to the point, enhance. Thus, "Phoenix," more directly:

BY THE TIME I GET TO PHOENIX SHE'LL BE RISIN',
SHE'LL FIND THE NOTE I LEFT HANGIN' ON HER DOOR.

SHE'LL LAUGH WHEN SHE READS THE PART THAT SAYS
    I'M LEAVIN',
'CAUSE I'VE LEFT THAT GIRL SO MANY TIMES BEFORE.

BY THE TIME I MAKE ALBUQUERQUE SHE'LL BE
    WORKIN',
SHE'LL PROB'LY STOP AT LUNCH AND GIVE ME A CALL.

BUT SHE'LL JUST HEAR THAT PHONE KEEP ON RINGIN'
OFF THE WALL,
THAT'S ALL.

BY THE TIME I MAKE OKLAHOMA SHE'LL BE SLEEPIN',
SHE'LL TURN SOFTLY AND CALL MY NAME OUT LOW,

AND SHE'LL CRY JUST TO THINK I'D REALLY LEAVE HER,
'THO' TIME AND TIME I'VE TRIED TO TELL HER SO,
SHE JUST DIDN'T KNOW
I WOULD REALLY GO.

The composer may sometimes depart from this kind of "map" of a song, but what both collaborators get is a mutual head start on realizing possibilities.

Punctuation is also critical in the lyric form—leaving out or putting in periods, commas, question marks, exclamation points, dashes, and more rarely colons and semi-colons, as well as employing them exactly. Not only in corresponding lines in each section of a song should they duplicate each other as completely as possible so that the composer may sustain and build his phrase-lengths and cadences, but even more, they indicate most specifically the thought processes in the line readings, of which the music will be an extension. The more attention to punctuation, the more accurately both sense and sound will be conveyed.

There is, thus, a kind of *lyric lead sheet* to construct. What occasionally intrudes is whether lyrics can be poetry. Two or three practical matters settle that. Poetry is written to be read or spoken, a lyric is written to be *sung*. Poetry is complete without explicit music, a lyric is incomplete without its explicit music. What cannot be emphasized enough is that a song is the aim. Some lyrics may approach poetry, as some poetry approaches lyrics, but when lyrics cross over to make music obtrusive or superfluous, the words are not lyrics; or when they require second hearings to make their impact, the words are not lyrics. If the lyricist gives his composer words in forms that "look like" poetry (my suspicion of the published version of "Phoenix" above), the working problems are worsened.

In the lyric form he chooses, the lyricist makes musical suggestions. Give the composer the best to improve upon.

Vocabularies

As for the words themselves, two vocabularies are at issue—the lyricist's and the characters'. The irony is that the wider the lyricist's vocabulary, and the truer his ear, the more voices he has; and the more the characters find all their voices, the more his voice comes through. The reverse hurts badly: if the characters sing in the lyricist's voice instead of their own, nothing of what the lyricist has to say is heard. The more observed, the more imaginable.

For **My Fair Lady**, Alan Jay Lerner, an upper-middle class, contemporary New Yorker, had to translate himself as lyricist (and bookwriter) to a 1912 London world. For all the advantage of Shaw's prior image of that world, Lerner was not relieved from creative effort of his own. On the contrary, he could have missed precisely for failing to re-absorb and thus re-create that world in his own vision.

Henry Higgins is still an upper class, comfortable professor of phonetics, and Eliza still a lower class, poor working girl; they are still thrown together into the middle of a class "tug-of-war," not knowing that each would end up tugging the rope between them. In the musical, however, the rope will become a lover's knot. At first, the "U"-speaking man sings in full hunting cry:

LOOK AT HER—A PRIS'NER OF THE GUTTERS:
CONDEMNED BY EV'RY SYLLABLE SHE UTTERS.
BY RIGHT SHE SHOULD BE TAKEN OUT AND HUNG
FOR THE COLD-BLOODED MURDER OF THE ENGLISH
    TONGUE! . . .

WHY CAN'T THE ENGLISH TEACH THEIR CHILDREN HOW
    TO SPEAK?
THIS VERBAL CLASS DISTINCTION BY NOW SHOULD BE
    ANTIQUE.
IF YOU SPOKE AS SHE DOES, SIR,
INSTEAD OF THE WAY YOU DO,
WHY YOU MIGHT BE SELLING FLOWERS, TOO . . .

By the time he has finished "Why Can't the English?," Higgins has displayed as much arrogance as wit and as much snobbery as erudition to establish himself as a model Englishman. Opposed immediately is a Cockney girl in her way as demanding:

ALL I WANT IS A ROOM SOMEWHERE,
FAR AWAY FROM THE COLD NIGHT AIR,
WITH ONE ENORMOUS CHAIR—
OH, WOULDN'T IT BE LOVERLY? . . .

Her model for a better world is more physical and "absobloomin-lutely loverly" than Higgins', but just as inventive and fervent. Both songs succeed, among other reasons, because the depth and detail of the idiosyncratic vocabularies reveals such specific characters.

Stephen Sondheim is also an upper-middle class, contemporary New Yorker, and familiar as lyricist (and composer) of **Company** with its 1970's New York world. Though he too was furnished with a particular image of it by a playwright, George Furth, from whose unproduced set of seven "mini-plays" **Company** was developed, Sondheim had to do his own creative research, too—into the world around him, and into his own experience.

Company opens with a title song ensemble number. It rises out of the 35th-birthday surprise party for Robert, which may not be very welcome to any of these over-30's, particularly Robert. To a different beat in a different world, Sondheim condenses character in the same economical way as Lerner—except here in fourteen individualized vocabularies. As detailed below, it begins with the five couples, then introduces Robert, then adds the three single girl friends, until all are finally united into an entire-company number that renders the musical's voice of New York richer, and Sondheim's voice clearer.

[The five couples are Jenny and David ("pot"), Peter and Susan ("divorced together"), Amy and Paul ("married after living together"), Joanne and Larry ("often-married") and Sarah and Harry ("karate").]

(Jenny)	BOBBY–
(Peter)	BOBBY–
(Amy)	BOBBY BABY–
(Paul)	BOBBY BUBI–
(Joanne)	ROBBY–
(Susan)	ROBERT DARLING–
(David)	BOBBY, WE'VE BEEN TRYING TO CALL YOU.
(Jenny)	BOBBY–
(Larry)	BOBBY–
(Amy)	BOBBY BABY–
(Paul)	BOBBY BUBI–
(Sarah)	ANGEL, I'VE GOT SOMETHING TO TELL YOU.
(Harry)	BOB–
(Larry)	ROB-O–
(Joanne)	BOBBY LOVE–
(Susan)	BOBBY HONEY–
(Amy and Paul)	BOBBY, WE'VE BEEN TRYING TO REACH YOU ALL DAY...

With increasing personal detailing, such as the characteristic names each has for Robert, and adding voices, this introductory verse builds to an ensemble climax, which is then topped by Robert's solo chorus:

(All)	BOBBY, COME ON OVER FOR DINNER!
	WE'LL BE SO GLAD TO SEE YOU!
	BOBBY, COME ON OVER FOR DINNER!
	JUST BE THE THREE OF US,
	ONLY THE THREE OF US,
	WE LOOOOOOVE YOU!

(Robert)   PHONE RINGS, DOOR CHIMES, IN COMES COMPANY!
             NO STRINGS, GOOD TIMES, ROOM HUMS, COMPANY!
             LATE NIGHTS, QUICK BITES, PARTY GAMES,
             DEEP TALKS, LONG WALKS, TELEPHONE CALLS,
             THOUGHTS SHARED, SOULS BARED, PRIVATE
               NAMES,
             ALL THOSE PHOTOS UP ON THE WALLS
             "WITH LOVE,"
             WITH LOVE FILLING THE DAYS
             WITH LOVE SEVENTY WAYS,
             "TO BOBBY, WITH LOVE"
             FROM ALL
             THOSE
             GOOD AND CRAZY PEOPLE, MY FRIENDS,
             THOSE
             GOOD AND CRAZY PEOPLE, MY MARRIED FRIENDS!
             AND THAT'S WHAT IT'S ALL ABOUT, ISN'T IT?
             THAT'S WHAT IT'S REALLY ABOUT,
             REALLY ABOUT!

Robert's choice of vocabulary is another model: the more personal, the more prototypal.

Enter Robert's three girl friends, April ("Barcelona"), Kathy ("Tick-Tock") and Marta ("Another Hundred People"). The number builds a second time, from solo lines to more varied group-ings, including those by sex and status (husbands, wives, singles). It again reaches the *climax* section above, adding the three extra voices (with appropriate changes: WE'LL/I'LL BE SO GLAD. . . , THREE/TWO OF US, WE/I LOOOOOOVE. . . , even though im-possible to hear). Then, still building, the entire company rides in on Robert's chorus (MY/YOUR FRIENDS . . .) to the grand climax:

(All)   . . .THAT'S WHAT IT'S REALLY ABOUT,
                      REALLY ABOUT!
(Husbands)   ISN'T IT? ISN'T IT? ISN'T IT?
(Wives and Girls) L O O O O O O V E!
(Husbands)   ISN'T IT? ISN'T IT? ISN'T IT?
(Robert)   YOU I LOVE AND YOU I LOVE AND YOU AND
                      YOU I LOVE
                   AND YOU I LOVE AND YOU I LOVE AND YOU
                      AND YOU I LOVE,
                   I LOVE YOU!

(All)   COMPANY! COMPANY! COMPANY,
                             LOTS OF COMPANY!
                             YEARS OF COMPANY! LOVE IS COMPANY!
                             COMPANY!

The lyrics of all three of these songs, "Why Can't the English?," "Wouldn't It Be Loverly?" and "Company," work because all the characters employ their specific languages to the fullest. These are then completed by music that further speaks their languages. Higgins sounds like a Higgins, Eliza like an Eliza, the New Yorkers like New Yorkers. "Why Can't the English?" puts all of Higgins' rhythmic power, dogmatism and acid wit into a mighty complaint, and proves how well he speaks. "Wouldn't It Be Loverly?" lifts Eliza's rhythmic ease, pragmatic self-serving, and creature-comfort day-dreaming into a delicious plea, and proves how much she yearns. The marrieds and the singles in "Company" are particularized in fourteen voices, but the varied vocabularies in concert typify a universal urban vocabulary. Caught in shibboleths like TRYING TO REACH YOU ALL DAY, WE'LL BE SO GLAD TO SEE YOU, JUST BE THE THREE OF US, WE LOOOOOOVE YOU, and catch phrases like LATE NIGHTS/QUICK BITES, DEEP TALKS/LONG WALKS, THOUGHTS SHARED/SOULS BARED, all those good and crazy people prove the changing chorus of all for one and one for all. Good lyricists are the relays, as it were, of every character in his or her own voice.

While vocabulary individuality is the starting point, lyrics sung must also be heard by the *collective* ear in a large hall (an auditorium is a "place of hearing"). Therefore all lyrics must furthermore be direct and immediate.

Direct: The words must strike the ear concretely, without abstractions or complications. This does not stop the lyricist from being witty, subtle or penetrating. Directness fosters sharpness, and images obviously make much suggestion.

Immediate: Whatever extra meanings they may hold, the words must count on impact. There is too much else going on for the eye (or the gut, heart or mind), and the ear is quickest to fall behind.

These two priorities produce two more. The lyrics must be vernacular and singable. *Singable* is so fundamental a requirement that it will take the largest part of the next chapter to implement it.

Vernacular: This is the *spoken* language native to a particular locality. It may take many forms. In the bar-room or the kitchen, the street or the farm, it may be as natural, pungent and earthy as the places themselves. In the living room or the nightclub, it may be as natural, barbed and elegant as the quickening of one's own pulse and wit at a good party. *Natural* is always relative to the context it happens in. Raw or polished, the vernacular is what gives color to language: the more lively, the more colors. A lyric is an epitome of how people speak in different circumstances, put to music.

In their inner variety as well as their overall contrast, four lyrics from the score of **My Fair Lady** and four from **Company** will present a digest of direct, immediate, vernacular and singable character vocabularies in lyric form. The four from **My Fair Lady** are Doolittle's two songs, his reprise of one, and Freddy's one song, to provide examples of the songs of a *character man* and a *leading man*.

Doolittle's first song is *verse-chorus* in feeling, fittingly the closest in style to *folk* music. It takes place outside his hangout, a tenement-neighborhood pub. The lyric is a toast, to the sly code of a working-class fortune-hunter before his "main chance" comes through:

> THE LORD ABOVE GAVE MAN AN ARM OF IRON
> SO HE COULD DO HIS JOB AND NEVER SHIRK.
> THE LORD ABOVE GAVE MAN AN ARM OF IRON—BUT
> WITH A LITTLE BIT OF LUCK,
> WITH A LITTLE BIT OF LUCK,
> SOMEONE ELSE'LL DO THE BLINKIN' WORK!

In only six lines, Doolittle arrives crafty, buffoonish, ready—and entire. Each word is personal, which sweeps everything before it, including one repeat for emphasis, the other for suspense.

A note about repetition in a lyric. It helps insure a song's idea, but it serves better purposes, as just noted, to increase the song's build; in this case, the usage capitalizes on the folksong form also, in which both repetition and the vernacular "common touch" are parts of the pleasure. In addition, repetition can channel strong emotions into strong actions. "I Could Have Danced All Night" and "Just You Wait!" in **My Fair Lady** and "Being Alive" in **Company** use repetition this way. The first turns joy into cheers, the second, anger into resolve, and the third, fear into affirmation. Repetition so used is a boost to the tight rhythms of comedy, and the big rhythms of passion, and doubtless has other applications. Unless highly purposive, however, an utterly simple repetition may also drag down, or cancel out.

Meanwhile back at the pub, two of Doolittle's pals "of the lowest possible class," Harry and Jamie, join in to make a trio of the "chorus" (recurring with changing tag lines):

WITH A LITTLE BIT, WITH A LITTLE BIT,
WITH A LITTLE BIT OF LUCK,
YOU'LL NEVER WORK!

The rest of Doolittle's "code" unfolds in the succeeding "verses":
how to get away with murder—be it work, liquor or women—each
of his punch-line tricks topping its predecessor. Besides being direct, immediate, vernacular and singable, now the lyrics must have
jokes that snap on the last line of the verse each time, and out-do
each other each time. The knack, à la Lerner and others, is to make
each joke advance character. Doolittle grows in craftiness and liveliness before our eyes and ears.

The *reprise* then pays off the character. Doolittle has found that
Eliza has had "a little bit of luck:" she has "moved in," he thinks,
with Higgins. The main chance!

A MAN WAS MADE TO HELP SUPPORT HIS CHILDREN,
WHICH IS THE RIGHT AND PROPER THING TO DO.
A MAN WAS MADE TO HELP SUPPORT HIS
    CHILDREN—BUT
WITH A LITTLE BIT OF LUCK,
WITH A LITTLE BIT OF LUCK,
THEY'LL GO OUT AND START SUPPORTING YOU! . . .

And "with a little bit of luck, he'll be movin' up to easy street."

When Doolittle shows up in Act II, however, the main chance
has not only made him rich, but is also about to hook him into
marriage. His code has slipped, and his raffishness is going fast. But
he rouses one last time.

I'M GETTING MARRIED IN THE MORNIN'!
DING, DONG! THE BELLS ARE GONNA CHIME!
PULL OUT THE STOPPER,
LET'S HAVE A WHOPPER,
BUT GET ME TO THE CHURCH ON TIME!

I GOTTA BE THERE IN THE MORNIN',
SPRUCED UP AND LOOKIN' IN ME PRIME.
GIRLS, COME AND KISS ME,
SHOW HOW YOU'LL MISS ME,
BUT GET ME TO THE CHURCH ON TIME! . . .

Through two complete choruses, a dance section, and a coda, with
jokes building to top each other again, the song telescopes and

transports Doolittle right through dawn to his doom. It is a build in reverse, Doolittle fading before us. Yet the words in idiom and rhythm and color are ever Doolittle, swaggering, staggering his way through adversity, a "pragmatic man." His "luck" has run out, but he goes down flying. And so do his big, round, easy-to-hear words.

Doolittle's two songs are rhythm tunes and, as noted earlier, could also be special material. Compounding the difficulty of writing a leading man's ballad for the character of Freddy is that "On the Street Where You Live" is his one song. The solution is all the bolder. Starting right with the verse, Freddy tries to adopt another character's language—Eliza's in her first "test" at Ascot:

> WHEN SHE MENTIONED HOW HER AUNT BIT OFF THE
>   SPOON,
> SHE COMPLETELY DONE ME IN.
> AND MY HEART WENT ON A JOURNEY TO THE MOON,
> WHEN SHE TOLD ABOUT HER FATHER AND THE GIN.
> AND I NEVER SAW A MORE ENCHANTING FARCE,
> THAN THE MOMENT WHEN SHE SHOUTED, "MOVE YOUR
>   BLOOMIN'—!"

Interruption! Mrs. Pearce, Higgins' housekeeper, opens the front door where Freddy is standing. But the audience has already learned more about Freddy from his trying to handle "the new small talk" than exposition could ever manage; indeed, trying for a clincher every two lines seals the perfectly caught awkwardness of his effort. Then he soars into his own fluent vocabulary in the chorus:

> I HAVE OFTEN WALKED DOWN THIS STREET BEFORE;
> BUT THE PAVEMENT ALWAYS STAYED BENEATH MY
>   FEET BEFORE.
> ALL AT ONCE AM I
> SEVERAL STORIES HIGH,
> KNOWING I'M ON THE STREET WHERE YOU LIVE....
>
> AND OH! THE TOWERING FEELING
> JUST TO KNOW SOMEHOW YOU ARE NEAR!
> THE OVERPOWERING FEELING
> THAT ANY SECOND YOU MAY SUDDENLY APPEAR!...

Instead of the push and bounce of Doolittle's vocabulary, Freddy's is a smoother, well-bred, upper-class idiom. It is also innocent, simple and straightforward, the hardest of all accomplishments. Yet it has extra suggestion, true of the best show songs. Ordinarily shy and ineloquent, Freddy is suddenly gifted beyond his powers; he finds words to match his worship. Of course Lerner the lyricist is at work, but by bringing out the most character he can in a straight man.

The four examples from **Company** comprise a female comedy trio, a young character woman's solo, a romantic duet, and a different leading man's song. The score in entirety again presents individual vocabularies musically and verbally, but it also presents a challenge to one of the four priorities. Sondheim's lyrics will sometimes be difficult to sing, and his music will sometimes compound that. The difficulties are not accidental, however, and Sondheim's answers to his own challenges may be instructive.

To the couple who are his squarest friends, Jenny and David, Robert is protesting his readiness for marriage. His three single girl friends sail in at the side, in group rebuttal, "You Could Drive a Person Crazy:"

DOO-DOO-DOO-DOO
DOO-DOO-DOO-DOO
DOO-DOO-DOO-DOO-DOO-DOO
YOU COULD DRIVE A PERSON CRAZY,
YOU COULD DRIVE A PERSON MAD.
DOO-DOO DOO-DOO DOO
FIRST YOU MAKE A PERSON HAZY,
SO A PERSON COULD BE HAD.
DOO-DOO DOO-DOO DOO
THEN YOU LEAVE A PERSON DANGLING SADLY
OUTSIDE YOUR DOOR
WHICH IT ONLY MAKES A PERSON GLADLY
WANT YOU EVEN MORE.

I COULD UNDERSTAND A PERSON,
IF IT'S NOT A PERSON'S BAG.
DOO-DOO DOO-DOO DOO
I COULD UNDERSTAND A PERSON,
IF A PERSON WAS A FAG.
DOO-DOO DOO-DOO DOO
DOO-DOO-DOO-DOO
BUT WORSE 'N THAT,
A PERSON THAT
TITILLATES A PERSON AND THEN LEAVES HER FLAT
IS CRAZY,
HE'S A TROUBLED PERSON,
HE'S A TRULY CRAZY PERSON HIMSELF!

(Simultaneous "ad libs")
You crummy bastard! . . . You son of a bitch! . . . You dirty
    bird-brain! . . .

(Kathy)
WHEN A PERSON'S PERSONALITY IS PERSONABLE,
HE SHOULDN'T OUGHTA SIT LIKE A LUMP.
IT'S HARDER THAN A MATADOR COERCIN' A BULL
TO TRY TO GET YOU OFF-A YOUR RUMP.
SO SINGLE AND ATTENTIVE AND ATTRACTIVE A MAN
IS EVERYTHING A PERSON COULD WISH,
BUT TURNING OFF A PERSON IS THE ACT OF A MAN
WHO LIKES TO PULL THE HOOKS OUT OF FISH.

(All three)
KNOCK, KNOCK, IS ANYBODY THERE?
KNOCK, KNOCK, IT REALLY ISN'T FAIR.
KNOCK, KNOCK, I'M WORKING ALL MY CHARMS.
KNOCK, KNOCK, A ZOMBIE'S IN MY ARMS.
ALL THAT SWEET AFFECTION,
WHAT IS WRONG?
WHERE'S THE LOOSE CONNECTION?
HOW LONG, OH LORD, HOW LONG?
BOBBY BABY, BOBBY BUBI, BOBBY,

YOU COULD DRIVE A PERSON BUGGY,
YOU COULD BLOW A PERSON'S COOL.
DOO-DOO DOO-DOO DOO
LIKE YOU MAKE A PERSON FEEL ALL HUGGY
WHILE YOU MAKE HER FEEL A FOOL.
DOO-DOO DOO-DOO DOO
WHEN A PERSON SAYS THAT YOU'VE UPSET HER,
THAT'S WHEN YOU'RE GOOD.
YOU IMPERSONATE A PERSON BETTER
THAN A ZOMBIE SHOULD.

I COULD UNDERSTAND A PERSON
IF HE WASN'T GOOD IN BED.
DOO-DOO DOO-DOO DOO
I COULD UNDERSTAND A PERSON
IF HE ACTUALLY WAS DEAD.
DOO-DOO-DOO-DOO
EXCLUSIVE YOU,
ELUSIVE YOU,
WILL ANY PERSON EVER GET THE JUICE OF YOU?
YOU'RE CRAZY,
YOU'RE A LOVELY PERSON,

YOU'RE A MOVING, DEEPLY MALADJUSTED,
NEVER TO BE TRUSTED
CRAZY PERSON
YOURSELF.

BOBBY IS MY HOBBY AND I'M GIVING IT UP.

A syncopated lyric by a writer who revels in word-games, Sond-heim expects singers and audiences to keep up with him. The lyric is explosively direct, immediate and vernacular, but almost not singable. It is a cataract of the densest, tightest sounds, taken at high speed, and by a trio in high female pitch (the hardest to hear and understand). But those are its marvels, because Broadway per-formers can master them to make the song a triumph. It deliberately makes the difficulties the assets. The trio becomes a *tour de force*: the contrasts of sounds, in strong syncopation (DOO-DOO DOO-DOO DOO) and part-singing (including *head* and *chest* voice "switches"), interweave to sweep everyone through the song. The crowning effect is seeing three girls in emotional orbit around Robert turn into a "sister" parody number.

Next, the lyric makes the idiomatic words even more idiomatic. In this case there are two idioms: New York snappers and female gnashes, combined in the very title: "You Could Drive a Person Crazy." A professional crossword puzzle maker, Sondheim seems to gather verbalisms into collections just to see if he can compose characters out of them. Thus, he likes to shake up clichés, as in all the phrases with PERSON. Then he plays on them more: PER-SONALITY, PERSONABLE, IMPERSONATE. Other plays on clichés are TURNING OFF; KNOCK, KNOCK; HOW LONG, OH LORD? and BLOW A PERSON'S COOL. He also likes to step up colloquialisms: COULD BE HAD, WHICH IT ONLY MAKES A PERSON, SHOULDN'T OUGHTA, LOOSE CONNECTION and GOOD IN BED . . . IF HE WAS DEAD. And he makes up words like HUGGY without fear, and rhymes like COERCIN' A BULL without shame.

He is expressive with non-words, too. The DOO's are more than rhythm breaks. Singly, they provide quotation marks, exclamation points, suspense or suggestion. Together, they put a maniacally cheerful surface on a maelstrom, the nuttiest effect of all. The con-tradictions at the end are most fitting: a boiling mass.

Moreover, the close-harmony plight of the three girls, all wound up about Robert, is a nice catch of *group* character. To focus and accent it, however, there is a spokeswoman: Kathy has a solo pas-sage in the middle of the number (its own obstacle to sing). The most "small town" of the three girl-New Yorkers, and the one who leaves to get married, Kathy, underneath the smart talk, expresses the most sensible view of Robert. Besides, the roles of Marta and April each have a big song, so Kathy, though primarily a dancing role, merits something of her own to sing. If there are inequalities of *distribution*, use them to lick them.

Marta, in "Another Hundred People," comes through just as acutely in her solo. An "observing" character, she sings her song as a "running moral" to her scene, which is in three parts: Robert on a park bench meeting first with April, then Kathy, then herself. The song opens the scene, then encores a complete chorus between April's departure and Kathy's arrival, then a half-chorus on Kathy's departure and her own involvement. It is all the more effective because in its one-and-a-half reprises there are no word changes but one, to be indicated. (Repeating the song this way, helping an audience to remember it while it forwards dramatic purpose, is also a neat trick.)

> ANOTHER HUNDRED PEOPLE JUST GOT OFF OF THE
>   TRAIN
> AND CAME UP THROUGH THE GROUND
> WHILE ANOTHER HUNDRED PEOPLE JUST GOT OFF OF
>   THE BUS
> AND ARE LOOKING AROUND
> AT ANOTHER HUNDRED PEOPLE WHO GOT OFF OF THE
>   PLANE
> AND ARE LOOKING AT US
> WHO GOT OFF OF THE TRAIN
> AND THE PLANE AND THE BUS
> MAYBE YESTERDAY.
>
> IT'S A CITY OF STRANGERS–
> SOME COME TO WORK, SOME TO PLAY–
> A CITY OF STRANGERS–
> SOME COME TO STARE, SOME TO STAY,
> AND EVERY DAY
> THE ONES WHO STAY
> CAN FIND EACH OTHER IN THE CROWDED STREETS AND
>   THE GUARDED PARKS,
> BY THE RUSTY FOUNTAINS AND THE DUSTY TREES AND
>   THE BATTERED BARKS.
> AND THEY WALK TOGETHER PAST THE POSTERED WALL
>   WITH THE CRUDE REMARKS,
> AND THEY MEET AT PARTIES THROUGH THE FRIENDS OF
>   FRIENDS WHO THEY NEVER KNOW,

WILL YOU PICK ME UP OR DO I MEET YOU THERE OR
  SHALL WE LET IT GO?
DID YOU GET MY MESSAGE? 'CAUSE I LOOKED IN VAIN.
CAN WE SEE EACH OTHER TUESDAY IF IT DOESN'T RAIN?
LOOK, I'LL CALL YOU IN THE MORNING OR MY SERVICE
  WILL EXPLAIN–

AND ANOTHER HUNDRED PEOPLE JUST GOT OFF OF THE
  TRAIN.
AND ANOTHER HUNDRED PEOPLE JUST GOT OFF OF THE
  TRAIN.
AND ANOTHER HUNDRED PEOPLE JUST GOT OFF OF THE
  TRAIN.
AND ANOTHER HUNDRED PEOPLE JUST GOT OFF OF THE
  TRAIN.

AND ANOTHER HUNDRED PEOPLE JUST GOT OFF OF THE
  TRAIN.

The one change reflects Kathy's departure (to leave and get married):

AND EVERY DAY
SOME GO AWAY
OR THEY FIND EACH OTHER . . .

The density, high voltage and momentum of this song make it also difficult to sing, so that its accomplishment is another feat. There are virtues in it, however, besides its fund of character in a vocabulary direct, immediate and vernacular. In spirit, the lyric is a round, spiraling around itself like a Laing "knot," and so is the action of the scene a round. It demonstrates how totally a song keys a scene in a good musical. Secondly, the New York ambiance—**Company**'s fifteenth character—or its first—finds special voice. It sounds through the entire lyric, Marta having become a prototypal young New Yorker, but most of all in the section on "finding each other." Paradoxes like RUSTY FOUNTAINS and DUSTY TREES, images like THE POSTERED WALL WITH THE CRUDE RE-MARKS, and the references to "meetings" and "messages" are, in fact, portrait painting, ordinarily to be discouraged in a show song but effective here because the action derives so much from the context.

The last **Company** examples are two of the *direct-action* songs. The first is Robert's and April's duet, "Barcelona." April is an airline stewardess. The two lovers are in bed, early in the morning. Exhausted.

(Robert)	WHERE YOU GOING?
(April)	BARCELONA.
(Robert)	...OH...
(April)	DON'T GET UP.
(Robert)	DO YOU HAVE TO?
(April)	YES, I HAVE TO.
(Robert)	...OH...
(April)	DON'T GET UP.
	NOW YOU'RE ANGRY.
(Robert)	NO, I'M NOT.
(April)	YES, YOU ARE.
(Robert)	NO, I'M NOT.
	PUT YOUR THINGS DOWN.
(April)	SEE, YOU'RE ANGRY.
(Robert)	NO, I'M NOT.
(April)	YES, YOU ARE.
(Robert)	NO, I'M NOT.
	PUT YOUR WINGS DOWN
	AND STAY.
(April)	I'M LEAVING.
(Robert)	WHY?
(April)	TO GO TO–
(Robert)	STAY–
(April)	I HAVE TO–
(Together)	FLY–
(Robert)	I KNOW–
(Together)	TO BARCELONA.
(Robert)	LOOK,
	YOU'RE A VERY SPECIAL GIRL,
	NOT JUST OVERNIGHT.
	NO, YOU'RE A VERY SPECIAL GIRL,
	AND NOT BECAUSE YOU'RE BRIGHT–
	NOT *JUST* BECAUSE YOU'RE BRIGHT.
	YOU'RE JUST A VERY SPECIAL GIRL,
	JUNE!
(April)	APRIL...
(Robert)	APRIL...
(April)	THANK YOU.
(Robert)	WHATCHA THINKING?
(April)	BARCELONA.
(Robert)	...OH...
(April)	FLIGHT EIGHTEEN
(Robert)	STAY A MINUTE.

(April)	I WOULD LIKE TO.
(Robert)	. . . SO? . . .
(April)	DON'T BE MEAN.
(Robert)	STAY A MINUTE.
(April)	NO, I CAN'T.
(Robert)	YES, YOU CAN.
(April)	NO, I CAN'T.
(Robert)	WHERE YOU GOING?
(April)	BARCELONA.
(Robert)	SO YOU SAID–
(April)	AND MADRID.
(Robert)	*BON VOYAGE.*
(April)	ON A BOEING.
(Robert)	GOOD NIGHT.
(April)	YOU'RE ANGRY.
(Robert)	NO.
(April)	I'VE GOT TO—
(Robert)	RIGHT.
(April)	REPORT TO–
(Robert)	GO.
(April)	THAT'S NOT TO SAY
	THAT IF I HAD MY WAY–
	OH WELL, I GUESS OKAY
(Robert)	WHAT?
(April)	I'LL STAY.
(Robert)	BUT–
	OH, GOD!

The seasaw lyric is still tricky, but compared to the two previous songs, this is a breeze to sing. The music floats the words, the early-morning moment: tired, tender, the polite and grateful host standing by, the proper and obliging guest moving on. Advancing, retreating, going through emotions, both go through the motions. The action of each makes the song go: interlaced negotiations in traded cadences: a true duet *exchange*: a scene. Words into music into drama.

Yet the words could not be simpler, the spoken casual ones and the unspoken loaded ones, with which to capture the hanging moment and the suspended couple. The lyric has a *dialogue naturalness*, of the same fabric as the dialogue, but in the most compact heightened shape. Indeed, all the examples from **My Fair Lady** and **Company** share this virtue of song as the acme of dialogue. It is surprising and unfortunate how often lyrics and dialogue may seem at odds with each other. Humor is one way of allying them; "Bar-

celona," a ballad with humor, is an example. Its far-out references
on one part and its tucked-in casualness on the other make the two
characters' vocabularies seem particularly natural counterparts, and
the one and two syllable words (instead of three or four syllable
words) make it seem effortless.

Robert's "Being Alive" is **Company**'s climax song. The much-
married Joanne, having scolded herself and "The Ladies Who
Lunch," suddenly propositions Robert, with the promise, "I'll take
care of you." He replies, "But who will I take care of?," and the
question shocks him. BOBBY BABY . . . (the verse of "Company")
resumes one last time, until Robert stops it midway with "What do
you get? " He starts his own answer:

> SOMEONE TO HOLD YOU TOO CLOSE,
> SOMEONE TO HURT YOU TOO DEEP,
> SOMEONE TO SIT IN YOUR CHAIR,
> TO RUIN YOUR SLEEP—
>
> SOMEONE TO NEED YOU TOO MUCH,
> SOMEONE TO KNOW YOU TOO WELL,
> SOMEONE TO PULL YOU UP SHORT
> AND PUT YOU THROUGH HELL—
>
> SOMEONE YOU HAVE TO LET IN,
> SOMEONE WHOSE FEELINGS YOU SPARE,
> SOMEONE WHO, LIKE IT OR NOT, WILL WANT YOU TO
>   SHARE
> A LITTLE, A LOT—
>
> SOMEONE TO CROWD YOU WITH LOVE,
> SOMEONE TO FORCE YOU TO CARE,
> SOMEONE TO MAKE YOU COME THROUGH,
> WHO'LL ALWAYS BE THERE, AS FRIGHTENED AS YOU,
> OF BEING ALIVE,
> BEING ALIVE, BEING ALIVE, BEING ALIVE.

And he paints himself into a corner. Helping are dialogue stings
around and about him from all the marrieds; they cut each stanza
short. All of a sudden, Robert breaks free—of the others and himself. He moves into the second chorus. It has very few word
changes, but the selectivity and subtlety of them produce an
enormous build:

> SOMEBODY HOLD ME TOO CLOSE,
> SOMEBODY HURT ME TOO DEEP,
> SOMEBODY SIT IN MY CHAIR

AND RUIN MY SLEEP AND MAKE ME AWARE
OF BEING ALIVE, BEING ALIVE.

SOMEBODY NEED ME TOO MUCH,
SOMEBODY KNOW ME TOO WELL,
SOMEBODY PULL ME UP SHORT
AND PUT ME THROUGH HELL AND GIVE ME SUPPORT
FOR BEING ALIVE, MAKE ME ALIVE,
MAKE ME ALIVE.

MAKE ME CONFUSED, MOCK ME WITH PRAISE,
LET ME BE 'USED, VARY MY DAYS,
BUT ALONE IS ALONE, NOT ALIVE.

SOMEBODY CROWD ME WITH LOVE,
SOMEBODY FORCE ME TO CARE,
SOMEBODY MAKE ME COME THROUGH,
I'LL ALWAYS BE THERE AS FRIGHTENED AS YOU,
TO HELP US SURVIVE
BEING ALIVE, BEING ALIVE, BEING ALIVE.

This second chorus is the full song. It completes the abortive first chorus, which was so defensive it never reached a release. A useful though difficult device mentioned earlier has worked: present a song in fragments or parts which are completed when the character comes together.

It is accomplished in this case by the technical skills of meter and rhyming. Throughout every individual word change, the meter is exactly retained: SOME<u>ONE</u> TO becomes SOME<u>BODY</u>, of <u>BEING</u> A<u>LIVE</u> matches the stresses of TO <u>HELP</u> US SUR<u>VIVE</u>, and so on, and all ride on the melody the same way. The cardinal change is the simplest, a main character transition by shifting from second person to first person: that is, from SOMEONE TO HOLD YOU TOO CLOSE to SOMEBODY HOLD ME TOO CLOSE. The pronoun shift is carried through the second chorus in rising force, crowned by the direct I'LL in place of WHO'LL near the end. Small details and crucial differences.

Internal rhyming is used to keep the first chorus punctuated (in the rhymes of SLEEP with DEEP, HELL with WELL), and to boost the second chorus (within the added *end* rhymes of AWARE and MY CHAIR, SUPPORT with SHORT). Internal rhymes are often employed for kicks, but here they keep the song together the first time around, and gather it to leap forward the second time. They also provide some extra meanings. The phrase TO HELP US SURVIVE in the second chorus last stanza can be taken on first hearing as a synonym for BEING ALIVE. But in context it also means "to survive being alive," the kind of wry pun very much in character for Robert to make.

The fulfillment of character occurs in the now arrived release. It is precisely where Robert takes the leap that brings him, in the very next line, first of the final A, to declare the word "love," thereby climaxing his recognition and acceptance of it, and pulling himself together.

Vocabulary equals character. "Being Alive"—one of Sondheim's most melodic and dramatic songs, in short and concrete words, packed with image and color—is direct, immediate, vernacular, and readily singable after all.

Titles

All the songs above work for an additional reason. Exactly what each one is about, its subject, is crystal clear, in the title—cue to the song's action.

The title may be the song's *springboard* ("With a Little Bit of Luck" and "Barcelona") or its *destination* ("Get Me To the Church on Time" and "Company") or its mainspring and *summary* ("Wouldn't It Be Loverly?" and "Sorry-Grateful"). But in all cases the title is the focus of the song. Moreover, its subject must deserve more than a dialogue line or two: it must inspire and justify an action that unrolls into an entire song. It must, however, contain one subject only; in the event there even seem to be two, one needs to subsume the other.

The title of an AABA, accordingly, will in general appear in the first A, usually at the beginning or the end of it, possibly in the second A but then in the same place—sometimes in the form of an *equivalent* of it (I COULD HAVE DANCED ALL NIGHT/I COULD HAVE SPREAD MY WINGS)—and almost certainly in the last A.

One place it may not appear, however, is in the B (unless it has already appeared earlier). The release is by definition transitional: if the title occurs there, the idea of the song is off target, the exact single subject still missing.

In an ABAC, the title will again appear in the first A, almost surely in the second A, possibly in the B as well, and even more surely in the C. In *verse-chorus*, the title may occasionally appear in the verse, but certainly appears in, and indeed carries, the chorus.

Assuredly, titles must be struggled for; only once in a while will the right one come right away. But it is mandatory to find it first, in order to write the song at all. It may come from trying different titles, seeing if the song develops out of one; or as the song evolves, the final title and thereby the final shape emerge. "Being Alive" evolved out of three earlier songs called "Marry Me a Little," "Multitudes of Amy" and "Happily Ever After."

Where the title actually appears, how often, if in any equivalents—these are the work specifics. It may fit best only once at the beginning, as in each chorus of "You Could Drive a Person Crazy" (page 129), the second time as an equivalent (YOU COULD DRIVE A PERSON BUGGY). It may appear only at the beginning and in different places in the middle, as in the two choruses of "Barcelona" (page 134). It may appear at the beginning, along the way as an equivalent, and at the end, as in "I Could Have Danced All Night." Or it may appear only at the beginning and the end, as in "The Ladies Who Lunch." The last is worth a look, for it will raise another point of interest about titles:

HERE'S TO THE LADIES WHO LUNCH–
EVERYBODY LAUGH.
LOUNGING IN THEIR CAFTANS AND PLANNING A
    BRUNCH
ON THEIR OWN BEHALF.
OFF TO THE GYM,
THEN TO A FITTING,
CLAIMING THEY'RE FAT
AND LOOKING GRIM
'CAUSE THEY'VE BEEN SITTING
CHOOSING A HAT–
DOES ANYONE STILL WEAR A HAT?
I'LL DRINK TO THAT.

HERE'S TO THE GIRLS WHO STAY SMART–
AREN'T THEY A GAS?
RUSHING TO THEIR CLASSES IN OPTICAL ART,
WISHING IT WOULD PASS.
ANOTHER LONG EXHAUSTING DAY,
ANOTHER THOUSAND DOLLARS,
A MATINEE, A PINTER PLAY,
PERHAPS A PIECE OF MAHLER'S–
I'LL DRINK TO THAT.
AND ONE FOR MAHLER.

HERE'S TO THE GIRLS WHO PLAY WIFE–
AREN'T THEY TOO MUCH?
KEEPING HOUSE BUT CLUTCHING A COPY OF *LIFE*
JUST TO KEEP IN TOUCH.
THE ONES WHO FOLLOW THE RULES,
AND MEET THEMSELVES AT THE SCHOOLS,
TOO BUSY TO KNOW THAT THEY'RE FOOLS–
AREN'T THEY A GEM?
I'LL DRINK TO THEM.
LET'S ALL DRINK TO THEM.

AND HERE'S TO THE GIRLS WHO JUST WATCH–
AREN'T THEY THE BEST?
WHEN THEY GET DEPRESSED, IT'S A BOTTLE OF SCOTCH
PLUS A LITTLE JEST.
ANOTHER CHANCE TO DISAPPROVE,
ANOTHER BRILLIANT ZINGER,
ANOTHER REASON NOT TO MOVE,
ANOTHER VODKA STINGER–
AAAAHH–I'LL DRINK TO THAT.

SO HERE'S TO THE GIRLS ON THE GO–
EVERYBODY TRIES.
LOOK INTO THEIR EYES AND YOU'LL SEE WHAT THEY
    KNOW:
EVERYBODY DIES.
A TOAST TO THAT INVINCIBLE BUNCH–
THE DINOSAURS SURVIVING THE CRUNCH–
LET'S HEAR IT FOR THE LADIES WHO LUNCH–
EVERYBODY RISE! RISE!
RISE! RISE! RISE! RISE! RISE! RISE! RISE!

The title might also be "I'll Drink to That." Not only might that
be too trite, however; "The Ladies Who Lunch" is far more a motor
for the song. The same things applies to "I'm an Ordinary Man."
There is a recurring line in that also, LET A WOMAN IN YOUR
LIFE?. None the less the first line, more propelling, holds as title.
Finally, both titles have a character reason behind them. "The
Ladies Who Lunch" is only a third person mask by which Joanne
lacerates herself. In "I'm an Ordinary Man," Higgins, in first person praise of himself, is equally egomaniacal:

I'M AN ORDINARY MAN . . .
AN AVERAGING MAN AM I . . .
JUST AN ORDINARY MAN . . .

> I'M A VERY GENTLE MAN . . .
> A PATIENT MAN AM I . . .
>
> I'M A QUIET LIVING MAN . . .
> A PENSIVE MAN AM I . . .
> JUST A QUIET LIVING MAN . . .

The choice also enabled the writers in both instances to wind the title around itself, in equivalents throughout the song, and around the audience.

The title appearing at the beginning, the middle and the end occurs in "Why Can't the English?" and "I've Grown Accustomed to Her Face." In such as these, its location forwards the song's development:

> I'VE GROWN ACCUSTOMED TO HER FACE!
> SHE ALMOST MAKES THE DAY BEGIN.
> I'VE GROWN ACCUSTOMED TO THE TUNE
> SHE WHISTLES NIGHT AND NOON . . .
>
> I'VE GROWN ACCUSTOMED TO HER LOOKS,
> ACCUSTOMED TO HER VOICE:
> ACCUSTOMED TO HER FACE.

Higgins interrupts his soliloquy with a comic explosion, but then the main song interrupts the explosion: the title wells in the music alone (a nice touch), verbally followed by:

> BUT I'M SO USED TO HEAR HER SAY
> GOOD MORNING EVERY DAY . . .

And then, the resolution:

> I'VE GROWN ACCUSTOMED TO THE TRACE
> OF SOMETHING IN THE AIR:
> ACCUSTOMED TO HER FACE.

In a shorter way, incidentally, the song makes the same use as in "Being Alive" of heightened internal rhyming (the extra rhyme of TRACE at the end) to extend the song's climax.

One song in **My Fair Lady**, surprisingly, has a title which doesn't appear at all: "A Hymn to Him." But a hymn to him is indeed its subject, and it generates the song:

> WHY CAN'T A WOMAN BE MORE LIKE A MAN?
> MEN ARE SO HONEST, SO THOROUGHLY SQUARE;
> ETERNALLY NOBLE, HISTORICALLY FAIR:
> WHO WHEN YOU WIN WILL ALWAYS GIVE YOUR BACK A
> PAT.
> WHY CAN'T A WOMAN BE LIKE THAT? . . .

This keeps on to its climax:

> WHY CAN'T A WOMAN BE MORE LIKE A MAN?
> IF I WERE A WOMAN WHO'D BEEN TO A BALL,
> BEEN HAILED AS A PRINCESS BY ONE AND BY ALL,
> WOULD I START WEEPING LIKE A BATHTUB
> OVERFLOWING?
> AND CARRY ON AS IF MY HOME WERE IN A TREE?
> WOULD I RUN OFF AND NEVER TELL ME WHERE I'M
> GOING?
> WHY CAN'T A WOMAN BE LIKE ME?

(The title otherwise keeps the song distinct from "Why Can't the English?.")

Its rhymes whipping, its title proven, "A Hymn to Him" calls for "Without You" as the retort necessary—the title indeed of the following song. Its rhymes cascading, it is of course sung by Eliza, now truly transformed. Not at the Embassy Ball but here is her main transition. It begins even in the introductory verse, then the chorus drives it home:

> WHAT A FOOL I WAS! WHAT A DOMINATED FOOL!
> TO THINK YOU WERE THE EARTH AND SKY.
> WHAT A FOOL I WAS! WHAT AN ADDLE-PATED FOOL!
> WHAT A MUTTON-HEADED DOLT WAS I!
> NO, MY REVERBERATING FRIEND,
> YOU ARE NOT THE BEGINNING AND THE END.
>
> THERE'LL BE SPRING EV'RY YEAR WITHOUT YOU.
> ENGLAND STILL WILL BE HERE WITHOUT YOU.
> THERE'LL BE FRUIT ON THE TREE,
> AND A SHORE BY THE SEA,
> THERE'LL BE CRUMPETS AND TEA
> WITHOUT YOU. . . .
>
> WITHOUT YOUR PULLING IT, THE TIDE COMES IN.
> WITHOUT YOUR TWIRLING IT, THE EARTH CAN SPIN.
> WITHOUT YOUR PUSHING THEM, THE CLOUDS ROLL BY.
> IF THEY CAN DO WITHOUT YOU, DUCKY, SO CAN I!

I SHALL NOT FEEL ALONE WITHOUT YOU.
I CAN STAND ON MY OWN WITHOUT YOU.
SO GO BACK IN YOUR SHELL,
I CAN DO BLOODY WELL
WITHOUT YOU.

A main transition may begin in the verse, incidentally, but the title can no more appear there than it can be in the B of an AABA. The verse is still the *situation*, the itch, and the chorus is still the *action*, the scratch. The chorus is where the title belongs, the song's identification. If the title comes up in the verse, anything from lead-in to the song's subject is still unfocused.

In passing, there is a song which has a theme or *text* for its title; in the trade, it is dubbed the *laundry list* song. It presents a catalogue of particulars, often for comedy purposes, sometimes for serious ones. Its examples range widely, from **The Sound of Music**'s "My Favorite Things" to **Kiss Me, Kate**'s "Where is the Life that Late I Led?" (WHERE ARE YOU, MOMO . . . LINA . . . ALICE . . . LUCRETIA . . . BECKY-WECCHIO . . . FEDORA . . . VENETIA . . . LISA?). In **My Fair Lady**, "Why Can't the English?," "I'm an Ordinary Man," "A Hymn to Him" and "Without You" might also be *laundry list* songs; in **Company** are "The Little Things You Do Together," "Getting Married Today" and "What Would We Do Without You?." But *laundry list* songs are not a class, the term is more playful than practical. They are a result of something basic, however: carrying a specific action through.

Accordingly, in sum, when the title is the first line, the song moves out from it; when it is the last line, the song moves in to it (if first and last, back to it); and when it is a repeated line, the song wraps around it.

The Implements of Show Lyrics

Rhyming
Meter
Phonetics

This section, like its predecessors, also proceeds from craft basics to the tools that carry them through. Those dealt with in this chapter may be the most precise so far.

This does not reduce the power of suggestion that words in the form of lyrics may make. On the contrary, the very precision enhances their power. "Content presents the task; form, the solution," German dramatist Friedrich Hebbel put it. When content and form are fused to the highest degree, the most powerful expression is achieved.

Conquering the difficulty of these last craft demands promises the greatest satisfactions.

144

Rhyming

Lyrics are words added up into unique shapes. Rhymes are what thread or nail this shaping, and what give the words point. They make the words easier to follow: they convey the idea even when one or two words may be missed, and insure hearing and remembering more of the words. To do these things, good rhymes do not accommodate the thought but pay it off, and at just the right place. Even in prose, in building strong statements to climaxes or in the feed-and-punch of jokes, that place is usually the last word or words. Lyrics go the last word one better—they rhyme it.

Technically, rhyme is matching the sounds of *stressed* syllables. "Theatricality" and "reality" is a rhyme, but "capacity" and "reality" is not, nor is "ability" and "reality": the stressed syllables do not match. Further, good rhymes make rhythms: long and short, slow and fast, regular and irregular; likewise they freshen words, even common ones, as bad rhymes depreciate them. For rhymes not only hold the lyric together but are often the juice of the song for the music to enhance. Again, the more discipline, the more expressiveness gained. Non-rhyming is not easier but harder, as will be touched on at the end of this segment.

All the songs in **My Fair Lady** and **Company** could serve as models—including the nonsense rhyming of "The Rain in Spain"—but "Show Me!" from the former and "The Little Things You Do Together" from the latter provide some extra pointers.

Back at the study, immediately following the triumph at the Embassy Ball, Higgins has totally ignored Eliza. On the street outside, however, Freddy waits to idolize her. He has begun his serenade. Eliza emerges and turns on him, the target at hand:

WORDS! WORDS! WORDS!   *(Verse)*
I'M SO SICK OF WORDS!
I GET WORDS ALL DAY THROUGH:
FIRST FROM HIM, NOW FROM YOU!
IS THAT ALL YOU BLIGHTERS CAN DO?

DON'T TALK OF STARS   *(1st Chorus)*
BURNING ABOVE.
IF YOU'RE IN LOVE,
SHOW ME!

TELL ME NO DREAMS
FILLED WITH DESIRE.

IF YOU'RE ON FIRE,
SHOW ME! . . .

DON'T TALK OF LOVE LASTING THROUGH TIME.
MAKE ME NO UNDYING VOW.
SHOW ME NOW!

This is Lerner's turn to overthrow clichés. Traditional terms of romance are stood on their heads, tenderness is turned into a howl. Some of the oldest rhymes of all come out new: ABOVE/LOVE and DESIRE/FIRE, made into such positive negatives, take on fresh life. This revitalizing is maintained throughout both choruses of the song. It is heralded in the verse: the last DO rhyme is also predictable, except that the line it concludes is so strong a turnabout from the two preceding *feed* lines, it surprises us anyway. There is another surprise at the end of the release in the second chorus:

NEVER DO I WANT TO HEAR ANOTHER WORD.
THERE ISN'T ONE I HAVEN'T HEARD.
HERE WE ARE TOGETHER IN WHAT OUGHT TO BE A
    DREAM.
SAY ONE MORE WORD AND I'LL SCREAM.

The rhyme of SCREAM/DREAM is as startling as it is unforced.

It is less the rhyme itself than how it gets there. The dull rhyme straggles home because the whole thought, not just the end word, is telegraphed. The bright rhyme zings home because it caps the thought, ahead of us. The beats in the line, the tempos they may be taken at—in sum, the balancing acts of rhythm from line to line— put further springs in the rhymes. This works so often in "Show Me!" that by the time the extensions at the end of each chorus arrive (the *first ending* is quoted above), the relief of a direct and obvious rhyme becomes preferable to any more surprise inventions. In show songs, the rhyming brings the character to a head.

Joanne starts "The Little Things You Do Together" during Robert's first scene with two of his married friends, Sarah and Harry, the "karate" couple. Like "Another Hundred People," it is another "running moral" to the scene. In this case, all the other couples join it before it is finished.

IT'S THE LITTLE THINGS YOU DO TOGETHER,
DO TOGETHER,
DO TOGETHER,
THAT MAKE PERFECT RELATIONSHIPS.

THE HOBBIES YOU PURSUE TOGETHER,
SAVINGS YOU ACCRUE TOGETHER,
LOOKS YOU MISCONSTRUE TOGETHER,
THAT MAKE MARRIAGE A JOY.
MM-HM –

IT'S THE LITTLE THINGS YOU SHARE TOGETHER,
SWEAR TOGETHER,
WEAR TOGETHER,
THAT MAKE PERFECT RELATIONSHIPS.
THE CONCERTS YOU ENJOY TOGETHER,
NEIGHBORS YOU ANNOY TOGETHER,
CHILDREN YOU DESTROY TOGETHER,
THAT KEEP MARRIAGE INTACT.

IT'S NOT SO HARD TO BE MARRIED,
WHEN TWO MANEUVER AS ONE;
IT'S NOT SO HARD TO BE MARRIED
AND, JESUS CHRIST, IS IT FUN.

IT'S SHARING LITTLE WINKS TOGETHER,
DRINKS TOGETHER,
KINKS TOGETHER,
THAT MAKES MARRIAGE A JOY.
IT'S BARGAINS THAT YOU SHOP TOGETHER,
CIGARETTES YOU STOP TOGETHER,
CLOTHING THAT YOU SWAP TOGETHER,
THAT MAKE PERFECT RELATIONSHIPS.

UH-HUH –
MM-HM –

(The other marrieds join Joanne)
IT'S NOT TALK OF GOD AND THE DECADE AHEAD THAT
    ALLOW YOU TO GET THROUGH THE WORST.
IT'S "I DO" AND "YOU DON'T" AND "NOBODY SAID THAT"
AND "WHO BROUGHT THE SUBJECT UP FIRST?"
IT'S THE LITTLE THINGS, THE LITTLE THINGS, THE
    LITTLE THINGS,
IT'S THE LITTLE THINGS, THE LITTLE THINGS, THE
    LITTLE THINGS,

THE LITTLE WAYS YOU TRY TOGETHER
CRY TOGETHER,
LIE TOGETHER,
THAT MAKE PERFECT RELATIONSHIPS.
BECOMING A CLICHÉ TOGETHER,
GROWING OLD AND GRAY TOGETHER,

(Joanne) WITHERING AWAY TOGETHER,
(All) THAT MAKES MARRIAGE A JOY.

(Men) IT'S NOT SO HARD TO BE MARRIED,
(Women) IT'S MUCH THE SIMPLEST OF CRIMES.
(Men) IT'S NOT SO HARD TO BE MARRIED.
(Joanne) I'VE DONE IT THREE OR FOUR TIMES.

(Jenny) IT'S PEOPLE THAT YOU HATE TOGETHER,
(Paul and Amy) BAIT TOGETHER,
(Peter and Susan) DATE TOGETHER,
(All) THAT MAKE MARRIAGE A JOY.

(David) IT'S THINGS LIKE USING FORCE TOGETHER,
(Larry) SHOUTING TILL YOU'RE HOARSE TOGETHER,
(Joanne) GETTING A DIVORCE TOGETHER,
(All) THAT MAKE PERFECT RELATIONSHIPS.

UH-HUH –
KISS, KISS –
MM-HM –

Where reversal was the surprise that sparked the rhyming in
"Show Me!," build is what sparks it in "The Little Things You Do
Together"—the title itself shows the way. At the beginning, the
triple repetition of DO TOGETHER establishes the pattern. The
contrasts of what marrieds "do together" then mounts through the
rhyme scheme, topped by the third line each time:

    . . . ENJOY TOGETHER
    . . . ANNOY TOGETHER
    . . . DESTROY TOGETHER

Each set equals or betters the preceding one, finally climaxed by
DIVORCE TOGETHER.
    Similarly, at the end of the first B section, AND, JESUS CHRIST,
IS IT FUN is a "shafter," yet it is out-done at the end of the second
B section by Joanne's I'VE DONE IT THREE OF FOUR TIMES.
The center C section, beginning IT'S NOT TALK . . . , sustains the
wit but provides a breather, to regather forces for the closing en-
semble singalong.
    Surprise is no less a feature of this lyric, too. The rhymes are so
natural, they achieve "inevitable surprise"—the ideal. "Another
Hundred People" is a similarly elaborated and ambitious song, but
"The Little Things You Do Together" as a longer song, and for
ensemble voices, proves the lyricist's lasting power and even

greater inventiveness. And in the typical Sondheim fashion of going himself one better, the song employs *feminine rhymes* (usually more difficult) not in couplets but triplets. A feminine rhyme is made up of words with *feminine endings:* that is, the last syllable is unstressed. TO<u>GETHER</u> is such a word. In "The Little Things," however, the main meaning—and musical stress—comes on the word directly preceding it:

> WINKS TOGETHER,
> DRINKS TOGETHER,
> KINKS TOGETHER . . .

Thus, the entire word TOGETHER falls off. The effect is of a three-syllable feminine ending in triplets.

The point leads to *Rhyme Schemes* in general, chief instrument of rhyming.

The root rhyme scheme is the *rhyme of* the *second* and *fourth* lines, or:

> a
> b
> c
> b

(Song forms, AABA, ABAC and so on, are indicated in UPPER CASE letters; rhyme schemes, a-b-c-b and so on, are indicated in lower case and hyphenated.) The "b" line is the only rhyme—the home port to return to regularly—giving aid and comfort, exactly so, to the ear. The a-b-c-b rhyme scheme is the germ from which all other rhyme schemes stem, including the two next basic, the *couplet* and *alternating rhymes:*

> a   a
> a   b
> b   a
> b   b

Fancier schemes follow, from the limerick (a-a-b-b-a) on.

Further, the overall pattern is the scheme. The rhyme-sounds in two matching sections of a song might literally be: a-b-c-b/d-e-f-e. But the scheme of that is a-b-c-b. Since the rhyme scheme will coincide with the song form (all the A's, for instance, will have the same rhyme scheme), it dictates the scheme of the song as a whole, with the usual exception of the release. The rhyme scheme will change there (and the meter as well) because the release must contrast musically, easiest to do if the verbal pattern also changes. Thus, the first chorus of "Being Alive" (page 136) starts out as a straight a-b-c-b. In the second and *completed* chorus (page 137), it becomes a-b-c-c-title, with the "left over" advantage of internal rhymes. The release is a couplet and a title-equivalent.

In turn, "You Could Drive a Person Crazy" (page 129) is a straight a-b-a-b, shifting only once to couplets, a scheme that holds throughout. The simplicity of the rhyme scheme makes the density of the song easier to follow (fostering in the complex staging the added parody of a "sister-trio"). "The Ladies Who Lunch" (page 139) performs another feat. It also begins as a straight a-b-a-b, but then varies it through the rest of the first section: a-b-a-b/ c-d-e/c-d-e/tag. The second section changes the scheme slightly: a-b-a-b/c-d-c-d/tag. The third changes it further: a-b-a-b/c-c-c/tag. But the fourth repeats the second, and the fifth and last repeats the third.

Rhyme schemes, too, are character.

Three couplet examples elaborate on rhyme schemes and their reflection of character. Thus, "I Could Have Danced All Night" is a-a-b-c-c-b, moves in the release to a-a, then concludes d-d-a. That middle couplet, however, requires a second look: it is *apocopated*. As written out in the original lyric form, it appears:

> I'LL NEVER KNOW
> WHAT MADE IT SO EXCITING,
> WHY ALL AT ONCE
> MY HEART TOOK FLIGHT.

Write the lines out, however, for the couplet they essentially are:

> I'LL NEVER KNOW WHAT MADE IT SO EXCITING,
> WHY ALL AT ONCE MY HEART TOOK FLIGHT.

The rhyme is of FLIGHT with EXCIT(E); the ING is hung out, as it were, behind the rhyme. This dropped or cut-off syllable is what is apocopated. The music seconds hearing the direct rhyme. Lerner apparently wanted insurance, though, so he adds internal rhyming: the entire word EXCITING is hung out or apocopated behind the rhyme of SO with KNOW, but then is picked up by FLIGHT in a reverse of apocopation, intensifying the rhyme, and the character response.

Apocopated rhymes are like "progressive" rhyming. They require great care, but occur in songs more frequently than is often realized.

"Barcelona" (page 134) is another such series of progressions, the most apocopated rhyming example in this book. It also combines internal rhyming; perhaps apocopation requires it. More to the point, however, is that under its elaborate yet casual exchanges, "Barcelona" is simply rhymed couplets! The discipline of the couplets is indeed what creates all the seesawing; the deliberate repetitions add to the naturalness; and the internal rhyme scheme buttresses the couplets and the couple.

As a third example, in "On the Street Where You Live" (page 128), the scheme is a-a-b-b-title throughout, and only the release relieves the couplets by switching to an a-b-a-b scheme. Yet alternating rhymes are also very regular. (The release may also be interpreted as a straight couplet with internal rhyming.) The song, of all the lyrics quoted, is the simplest, most obvious example of regularized rhyming, to go with Freddy, the simplest, straightest character.

If there can be couplets, there can also be triplets: "The Little Things You Do Together" (page 146) is a-a-a-b, and "Without You" (page 142) is a couplet and a triplet. "Wouldn't It Be Loverly?" (page 122) is a-a-a-title.

The release of "Wouldn't It Be Loverly?" introduces a *neologism*, ABSOBLOOMINLUTELY; LOVERLY is one in the first place. *Neologisms* are new or made-up words, or new uses of existing words, or phrases. They too must be revelations of character, not just tricks, and when successful they rediscover language. They are obviously a lyricist's delight, and few lyricists worth their salt do not try them. (They are a pleasure and speciality of E.Y. "Yip" Harburg's lyrics, in **Finian's Rainbow, Bloomer Girl, Jamaica**, the film **The Wizard of Oz**, and elsewhere. Harburg, by the way, has an apt definition of a song: "The music is the wings, the words the destination; songs are a vehicle to 'feel thoughts.'") Neologisms sometimes lead to treats of rhymes not otherwise attainable, employing a verbal nimbleness never to be found in a rhyming dictionary:

AN ENGLISHMAN'S WAY OF SPEAKING ABSOLUTELY
    CLASSIFIES HIM.
THE MOMENT HE TALKS HE MAKES SOME OTHER
    ENGLISHMAN DESPISE HIM.

Rhyming dictionaries can in fact inhibit or deflect a lyricist's playfulness and originality. Other examples:
"You Could Drive a Person Crazy" (page 129) has WORSE 'N

THAT/PERSON THAT, UPSET HER/BETTER and, already noted, BUGGY/HUGGY. There are more extended ones:

> WHEN A PERSON'S PERSONALITY IS PERSONABLE,
> HE SHOULDN'T OUGHTA SIT LIKE A LUMP.
> IT'S HARDER THAN A MATADOR COERCIN' A BULL . . .

If that one is hard to get, the next one is easy:

> EXCLUSIVE YOU,
> ELUSIVE YOU,
> WILL ANY PERSON EVER GET THE JUICE OF YOU? . . .

(These are also called *mosaic* rhymes, two or more words used to rhyme with one.)

From Lerner's **Camelot** this time, first from "The Simple Joys of Maidenhood":

> SHALL I NOT BE ON A PEDESTAL,
> WORSHIPPED AND COMPETED FOR?
> NOT BE CARRIED OFF, OR BETTER ST'LL,
> CAUSE A LITTLE WAR?

Second, from "The Lusty Month of May":

> IT'S MAY! IT'S MAY!
> THE MONTH OF "YES, YOU MAY,"
> THE TIME FOR EV'RY FRIVOLOUS WHIM,
> PROPER OR "IM." . . .
>
> IT'S MAY! IT'S MAY!
> THE MONTH OF GREAT DISMAY,
> WHEN ALL THE WORLD IS BRIMMING WITH FUN,
> WHOLESOME OR "UN."

Granted, neologisms are difficult and dangerous. That may be why, when they are successful, they are de-lovely.

Another kind of neologism may be, to coin a term, *implied* rhymes. The first example comes from the close of Freddy's verse to "On the Street Where You Live":

> AND I NEVER SAW A MORE ENCHANTING FARCE,
> THAN THE MOMENT WHEN SHE SHOUTED, "MOVE YOUR
>   BLOOMIN'—!"

Interruption in the nick of time; in more shows than one, some rhymes depend upon it. *Euphemism* is another example of the same thing, as in Eliza's "Without You":

YOU, DEAR FRIEND, WHO TALK SO WELL,
YOU CAN GO TO HERTFORD, HEREFORD AND
HAMPSHIRE!

First cousin to *implied* rhymes, to coin more working terms, are *dropped* rhymes, or *surprise non-rhymes.* Often a feature of light verse, they occur when the expected rhyme is intercepted, and succeed when the rhyme and rhythm are so predominant, the non-rhyme break is a pleasure. Thus, in the middle of "Why Can't the English?", Higgins suddenly drops the beat for:

THE FRENCH NEVER CARE WHAT THEY DO, ACTUALLY, AS
LONG AS THEY PRONOUNCE IT PROPERLY.

Going things one better again, both the opening and closing sections of "You Could Drive a Person Crazy" (page 129) build all the way to dropping the final rhymes.

"Side by Side by Side" has the most original *dropped* rhyme. The number is written to be staged in its straw-hat-and-cane grand finale in vaudeville fashion, with the five couples, Robert in the middle, lined up *in one* across the stage. Each couple does a brief tap step "dialogue": one starts the step, the other finishes it. When the dialogue reaches Robert, there is no one there to answer him. In the quick silence, to the beat, a "physical" rhyme, not just a verbal one, is dropped.

Dropped rhymes obviously depend on the rest of the lyric staying very strict, and only fit certain characters or situations.

The last rhyming classification has already been cited several times, *internal* rhyming (or *interior* rhyming). The *chorus* of "Company" (page 124) provides the fullest overall example in this book. Internal rhymes are of course rhymes within the lines, in addition to the *end rhymes.* They perform such pleasing feats— tightening, highlighting, enlivening—that there is a constant temptation to overuse them and thus to weaken their effectiveness. Yet most lyricists early in their career find them irresistible, until they accept that character in action is what everything must first obey.

Incidental to internal rhyming is *alliteration*. The *verse* of "Company" (page 123) is a good example. Alliteration fits poetry better in general, however, than it does lyrics in particular, which has music to heighten the words and does not need literary bracing. From the composer's viewpoint, in fact, alliteration needs to prove a super-asset, otherwise it is a liability.

All examples have been of *perfect* (or *full*) rhymes. These are rhymes in which vowels, consonants and stresses echo each other exactly. There are also *imperfect* (or *near*) rhymes, which once again fit poetry better, where the eye helps, than when the ear is all. There is in fact an entire catalogue of them, deliberately omitted because all are literary, not aural. The imperfect kind of rhyme that does occasionally appear are such pairs as "time/mine," for want of a neater solution, or "man/hand," sounds that may be elided.

Here are some concluding illustrations of how rhyme schemes fit character while they make music. The rhyme schemes in Doolittle's two songs, different cuts from the same cloth, reveal even more sharply how character-packed they are. "With a Little Bit of Luck" (page 126) literally is a-b-repeat a (apocopated)-title-title-b, but reduced to fundamentals it is a-b-a-c-c-b. "Get Me To the Church on Time" (page 127) is a-b-c-c-b. In other words, it is the same with one less line, and both c's are even short lines. Again, what is apparently complex works by the simplest rhyme schemes.

"I'm an Ordinary Man" moves from chorus sections in an appropriately easy, ad lib style with enough rhyming here and there to hold them together, to verse sections of the strictest and most compressed rhyming: precisely through that compression, Higgins explodes, emotionally and verbally. The lyric in the freest form of all, "I've Grown Accustomed to Her Face," is held closely together in its middle section by rhymed couplets of varying length, but is sustained in its entirety by its easy, cadence-rhymed musical lift—all of which dramatizes Higgins' final loosening up.

All the surface intricacies, lastly, of both "Why Can't the English?" (page 122) and "Barcelona" (page 134) are controlled by the simple use of rhymed couplets, expressing in one case powerful self-assertiveness, in the other, the politest coming together.

These analyses are all after the fact, yet so are rhyme schemes themselves. That is, they are a result of process, they do not start out by prescription. They arrive because they seem to fit and develop character. Sensing them is intuitive, but once they begin to work the scheme forms and then sees the song through.

There are incidental helps. If the rhyme is predictable, surprise may be achieved by a twist in getting there. "Charms/arms" is a cliché's cliché. In "You Could Drive a Person Crazy," the solution is:

KNOCK, KNOCK, I'M WORKING ALL MY CHARMS.
KNOCK, KNOCK, A ZOMBIE'S IN MY ARMS.

If the rhyme is obvious, proceed anyway if it is going somewhere and helps to get there. Not every line has to be a knockout. Besides, brand new meanings may come along: "June/moon" is fresh again for the space age. If, however, the rhyme is too bland or flat, there may be images that are missing or too general, or terms too passive or abstract. Active and concrete words make better music, too.

The danger is letting the rhyme make the meaning, of using words to match a sound at the cost of the intent or, worse, for want of one. This is why rhyming dictionaries may throw more water than coal on the fire. Rhyming is word play, but the stakes are higher than a game. The way to meet this is by total pre-planning. Determine thoroughly beforehand what the lyric should say, and hold to it except for a better idea. Indeed, go so far as to write it out fully in prose first, section by section, and *then put that to rhyme.* Flexibility is another strength. Instead of struggling, for instance, for the one word that makes the rhyme, a willingness to throw out the whole line or set of lines and recast the thought anew often is a better solution.

Every way of keeping rhyme the servant to the purpose must be found, because rhymes are the capstones that make words into music into drama, and songs into scenes. Rhymes set up forward motion, bring it regularly to peaks, score points. Indeed, they spotlight character, so to speak, by compacting the character's rhythms—a verbal beat to help the musical beat key the character action. Their power is formidable as means, not meanings. Do not say what rhymes, rhyme what you want to say.

Non-rhymed lyrics have had something of a vogue, especially under some of the liberating influence of contemporary pop music, but they bring special problems to show songs. In **Hair,** for instance, rhyme is frequently thrown to the winds, but only sometimes effectively. Its clearest success is "Frank Mills," whose *run-on prose* dramatizes the still formless budding of the innocent girl who sings it. (The music in AABA of course rhymed very strictly instead.) At first, however, rock show lyrics lost themselves not only in a zeal of faith and protest, but even more in the amplified sound which engulfed the words. The sensation was all the sense. The resulting dramatic slack had its momentary compensation in orgiastic exhilaration, a primeval power of theater. But drama gets back into theater all the time. Its return to contemporary lyrics in musicals re-individualized show lyrics too, as in the fresh and richly systematized rhyme-scheming of **Jesus Christ Superstar.**

Unrhymed lyrics were used as an *invention* in musicals before **Hair,** to be sure, though unlike **Hair,** without successors. In **The Music Man,** "Rock Island" (the "railroad" song opening the show sung *a cappella* by all the traveling salesmen) and "Ya Got Trouble" are outstanding examples. Even Lerner once wrote unrhymed lyrics: "I Talk to the Trees" in **Paint Your Wagon,** and most of its opening number, "I'm on My Way."

In every one of these cases, however, such choices were made because character and situation dictated it as the most suitable; above all, the lack of rhyme was *compensated for.* Not only were *repetitions* and *internal rhyming* substituted; even more, strongly rhythmic phrasing made up completely for the absence of rhyme. As rhyme defines rhythm, rhythm may make its own rhymes.

Meter

Meter and *phonetics* complete the definition of rhyming. They are inseparable, taken up in order here merely for convenience.

Meter is the pattern of accents (or stresses) in the rhythm. The first song in the previous chapter, "By the Time I Get to Phoenix" (page 119), has an irregular meter. Scan some of the lines (those that *correspond* to each other in each stanza), and they will be seen to have differing numbers of syllables, occasionally justifiable, but pushing and straining in many places against the natural fall of the accents. As a result the irregularity requires changes in note values throughout the song, from half notes to eighths to ties, around the downbeat and the secondary accents. The musical notation, in fact, differs in its three choruses every time. In just the following corresponding lines, with main accents indicated (/), note all the accommodations:

```
        /                        /                           /
    SHE'LL  FIND THE NOTE I LEFT  HANG-IN'      ON  HER  DOOR
    SHE'LL  PRO- B'LY    STOP AT LUNCH      AND GIVE ME   A    CALL
SHE'LL TURN  SOFT-  LY     AND CALL         MY NAME  OUT  LOW
```

In contrast, scan corresponding lines in "Sorry-Grateful" (page 22), and they match exactly every time. The syllables, accents and note values all fall in the same places throughout:

```
         /                /             /           /
    YOU'RE  AL- WAYS    WON- D'RING  WHAT  MIGHT  HAVE BEEN,
    THEN    SHE WALKS   IN.

    YOU     HOLD HER    THINK-ING   I'M    NOT    A-  LONE,
    YOU'RE STILL A-     LONE.
```

While it is true that jazz and rock have loosened up the rigidities of regular meters, in show songs this can go only so far. The free and easy, deliberately unstrict *folk-pop* style that helps "Phoenix" succeed in its terms is precisely what would make it fail as a show song. It is too personal a statement by the songwriter (especially as his own performer) to make character points, or to build tightly, or to serve additional score uses—all show song essentials.

"Sorry-Grateful" demonstrates the *show time* strength by which strict form increases the content. The first two A sections are exact musical repeats, while the words build. The effect is to make the words easier to hear at the same time that they heighten suspense. Some current pop songwriters—and many novice show songwriters—misjudge the power of musical repetition, fearing it is dull. On the contrary, such repetition heightens the feeling of release the B section provides, leading to a greater climax. Note how the first chorus ending of "Sorry-Grateful" is extended in the second and final chorus ending (enhanced by the music which in this instance becomes more tender). Pop songs do not intensify in the same way, especially in their lyrics. The *rhythms* of words make music make drama.

The key lies in the main accents of a song—the first beat, or *downbeat*, in each measure. They are the rhythm's anchors, or the bases the song moves along. Since the downbeats hold the song together precisely while they move it along, they are the places for the *key words* in the lyric to fall. Matching their stresses in the same place throughout is a chief means by which a lyric underpins and builds its impact. When sung lyrics are blurred, that may in turn be due to slurring the downbeats.

Today, it is true, some accents vary more from the downbeat, especially exaggerated and displaced accents. Calypso music does it continuously. Bock and Harnick do it in **Fiorello!** in a song title, by changing the word the downbeat falls on:

/   /   /
I LOVE A COP—I LOVE A COP.

Johnny Mercer did it, famously, for the film **Daddy Long Legs**, in which the downbeat and the vitality both progress:

/   /
SOMETHING'S GOTTA GIVE, SOMETHING'S GOTTA GIVE,
                        /
SOMETHING'S GOTTA GIVE.

Even livelier is the downbeat accent which the music takes but the words skip, as in "Big Spender," **Sweet Charity**, and "Everything's Coming Up Roses," **Gypsy**. It takes clear aim and skill, however, for the sense to spring off the meter and the music.

The stress within words is the elemental key to meter; hearing the different stresses is more important than knowing their names.

◡/	short-long, or		
	unstressed-stressed	"be<u>come</u>"	(iamb)
/◡	long-short	"<u>come</u>ly"	(trochee)
◡◡/	short-short-long	"over<u>come</u>"	(anapest)
/◡◡	long-short-short	"<u>com</u>pany"	(dactyl)
◡/◡	short-long-short	"be<u>com</u>ing"	(amphibrach)
/◡/	long-short-long	"<u>com</u>ing <u>through</u>"	(amphimacer, cretic)
//	long-long	"<u>come on</u>!"	(spondee)
◡◡	short-short	"in a," "to the"	(pyrrhic)-often,

however, combined with another word to make an anapest or a dactyl

("Become comely. Overcome company in a becoming coming-through. Come on!")

Meters also come in *feet:* the number of stresses to a line. If the words "come on" were the whole line, it would be a *dimeter* (two stresses, or a two-foot line). "Come to me, my melancholy baby" is a *pentameter*. Further, when the last syllable of a word (or a line) is stressed, it has a *masculine ending* ("become"); unstressed, a *femining ending* (comely").

Every single meter cannot be labeled exactly, however. Professional scanners—prosodists—debate endlessly over some lines. But clear metrical awareness between lyricist and composer can quicken each other's work. "Why Can't the English?" turns out to be difficult not for its rhyme scheme (couplets), but for its meter. Yet the solution is only a matter of knowing how to take liberties without taking license. Overall, the meter is very strict. When the meter is broken, consequently, it is in order to score. But the departures from strictness are even more condensed to emphasize strictness. The result is an effect of that formidable form, light verse—such as the line deliberately thrown away *ad lib* right in the metronomic middle; IN AMERICA, THEY HAVEN'T USED IT [English] FOR YEARS! In four more lines, the effect is not only repeated but topped, as it has to be; it is longer in length and its impending rhyme is denied, or "dropped": THE FRENCH NEVER CARE WHAT THEY DO, ACTUALLY, AS LONG AS THEY PRONOUNCE IT PROPERLY. The crowning touch is the way the music refines the meter. Precisely for its presto tempo, the downbeats set off the key words incisively.

Phonetics culminates these workings of meter.

Phonetics

Phonetics make the chosen accents sound out. In opera the vowels count far more than the consonants (in whatever language), but in musical theater they emerge together. The vowels make the sounds to sing by, but the consonants around them make the sounds signify.

The basic vowel question is one of *open* and *closed* sounds. All the vowel sounds come from certain parts of the mouth (from back to front), depending on the positions of the tongue (from high in the mouth to low), and simultaneous relaxings or tensings of the other speech organs (throat, lips, and so on). Thus, for a back-vowel, low-tongue sound like *ah* in "doll," all the organs are loose; for a front-vowel, high-tongue sound like *ee* in "see," they are tight. For the singer, the *ah* is an *open* sound, the *ee* a *closed* sound.

And for the lyricist and the composer! Since vowels are the means of exhaling, the more open ones are better for higher or sustained notes. There are some quick exceptions to this. Different voices work differently, as do the male and female voices generically; so do *head* and *chest* resonances, and there are also vocal techniques that compensate. Specific dramatic purposes make other demands. Yet this principle is still the point of departure. Exceeding its limits results in the vocal wrench of O'ER THE LAND OF THE FREEEE—the most closed vowel sound posted on the melody's top, prolonged and indeed climactic note. (The fault was bad collaboration, or non-collaboration. The words were placed directly over a contemporary English drinking song, "To Anacreon in Heaven.") Closed sounds are the hardest to reach, articulate or sustain.

Even if the melody rises only here and there, words with open vowel sounds work better. Success in finding them is not always possible, but composer and lyricist may abet each other greatly in this regard. Not only may the composer be so alive to sounds that he can contribute apt words, he can also put words on a melody in several ways, riding easily on the fluent sounds and overcoming some of the difficult ones. (Unless this constricts him; if he must repair, he cannot enhance.) The lyricist may with equal deftness be able to adapt to a given musical idea, and contribute devices for it.

A case in point is "On the Street Where You Live" (page 128), the most *vocal* male ballad in **My Fair Lady**. Where the words and phrases are very singable, the tones and cadences augment them; where less singable, they ease them. OF-TEN WALKED, thus, are similar sounds which are fairly free and open: the melody can rise easily on them. STREET is more difficult, a tenser, closed sound, full of friction: but that is disguised because the melody goes down rather than up, every time the word arrives. In the third line, AM I leaps an interval of a 7th, and holds for four beats on the I, another closed vowel sound. Ordinarily it would be hard to sing. But it is prepared for by the more open vowel sound of the directly preceding AM, which leaps first. Finally, on the following line, which is dominated by more closed vowel sounds (I'M, STREET, YOU, LIVE), the lyricist helps in turn. The *oh* sound of the first word, KNOWING, and the *ah* sound of the third word, ON, are two of the most open sounds available: they clear the channel, as it were, for the difficulties. "Singableness" in practice is what lyricist and composer do coordinately for vowels and consonants.

The following compilation of the vowel sounds is a starting point.

Open vowel sounds: A as in bah, ago
                          O as in go, oh, odd, out
                            (diphthong), too
                          U as in tub, true

Closed vowel sounds:	A as in say (diphthong)
	E as in see, dear (diphthong)
	I as in it, my (diphthong)

Mid vowel sounds:	A as in care, call, cat
	E as in hen, heard, her
	I as in first
	O as in boy (diphthong), book, word
	U as in full, fur, fuel (diphthongs)

Few vowel sounds stay pristine, however. Certain consonants before or after them cause changes in their sounds. Further shadings come from context, when words are put together; in addition, there are the myriad speech differences. (Composer Kenneth Jacobson, my workshop and professional colleague, comes from Maine. It was not until he came to New York, he says, that he found out that "farm" and "calm" do not rhyme.) But a more important change happens to the vowels aloud as dramatic circumstances alter their tones: rising or falling inflections, tender or driving rhythms—a host of changing effects. In show songs, acme of all this, these tone changes are precisely what is shaped to be sung; the tones become the tunes, so to speak.

True, singers may sometimes contribute to solving the difficulties of some high, closed vowel sounds (opening them, for instance, into diphthongs). But vocal solutions are not writing solutions. None the less, the more both composer and lyricist know about vocal production, the more resourceful their songs will be.

The vowel by itself is only part of the sound of the word, and less of the sense. Consonants need to be easy to hear, too. They can elide into jumbles, however, like the "t's" in "the night time" (lapsing into "the night I'm" or "the nigh time"); similarly, the "s's" in "this single moment," or (in "My Best Girl" in **Mame**) the "f's" in "rough for me" and "enough for me." To be clear, all such cases require the singer to stop short to cut the *liaisons*—unnecessarily awkward. "S" in general is not the most musical of sounds, and Lerner says he goes back over a lyric to try to remove words with it. Other difficult or non-musical sounds *to sing* might be "sts," hard "g," or middle or end sounds like "th" or "ch." But everyone has his own such catalogue, which also extends to words, such as "ghastly," "breath," "grudge," "stretched," "flop," and so on. One's own ear rejects them, or makes them into challenges. (What can I do with "Krupke?")

In "Another Hundred People" (page 132), there are some combinations of words which, at fast tempo, are all the harder to sing—BATTERED BARKS, THE POSTERED WALLS, SEE EACH OTHER TUESDAY, SERVICE WILL EXPLAIN—but they are purposive parts of Sondheim's style. By the same token, Lerner pointed out that he once chose harsh sounds and rhythms for dramatic purposes, expressly to slow down and flatten out the music. The finish of Guenevere's last song in **Camelot,** "I Loved You Once in Silence," goes:

> AND NOW THERE'S TWICE AS MUCH GRIEF,
> TWICE THE STRAIN FOR US,
> TWICE THE DESPAIR,
> TWICE THE PAIN FOR US,
> AS WE HAD KNOWN BEFORE.

The round, open sounds at the very end, however, sure enough break through the dam of the bleak sounds. "A fastidious ear and a simple heart should be the best combination," prescribes actress Athene Seyler for period acting in her book, *The Craft of Comedy.* It is the best recommendation for lyric writing, too.

What began in the previous chapter as a visual lyric form ends here as an aural lyric form. A lyricist cannot be more sure than by reading his lyrics *aloud* to his composer, and his composer to him, back and forth, often. The phonetics and the meters, the rhymes, the tempos and the idiosyncratic vocabularies—in sum, the character rhythms—will come through to both of them ever more and more sharply. The sound will be the sense heightened, the song will be the voice of the action. Words to make music to make drama.

Production

The Presentation
The Creative Staff
Rehearsal and Tryout
The Money, and Other Rewards

The most exhilarating and toughest parts are still to come.

First of all, a producer who will finance and get the musical on must be found. This requires a *presentation*.

If it succeeds in gaining a producer, one of his first steps will be to bring in a new set of collaborators. This is the *creative staff*.

Then, while money-raising is going on, theaters are negotiated for and other business matters are arranged, actors are auditioned and the musical is cast. It goes into rehearsal and moves on to the tryout. The New York opening lies ahead.

During every stage, the rewriting has never stopped but grown more intensive and exhausting. Every stage instructs, for better or for worse.

If all goes well, however, there are unheard-of money rewards. There may also be other compensations.

The Presentation

The musical's writers must now become what shocks many writers and few are ready for: its salesmen. Peddlers is a better word. This is not open to choice. Absolutely no one else will sell a first musical. An agent cannot sell it to a producer unless the agent is sold first. The writers will need every resource they can develop: contacts, workshops, cleverness, doggedness, *chutzpah.*

A *presentation* is the first step. It is a huge job: a new show must be made of the show just written. Featuring a few selected songs, it must be *packaged* into a compact form so lively as to make a producer want to produce the complete musical. Further, a musical makes the rounds of New York producers in an entirely different fashion from a straight playscript. The latter speaks for the playwright, but for a musical its writers speak for it in person, by playing and singing its package version *live,* with or without other performers. (Even for subsequent new musicals, the writers still do presentations live.) Nine times out of ten, the book of a musical is read by a producer only if the songs have prompted interest first.

A new playscript is hard enough to read and judge properly. But it is almost impossible to read a new musical properly. The appearance of the bare lyrics on the page, the relatively "telegramatic" dialogue sections, the quick alternations of characters and scenes, the token indications of production numbers, seem sketchy or confusing. All scripts are only blueprints for performance; reading a musical is the hardest blueprint of all, and even seasoned professionals have difficulty. (Tapes are no substitute, can be misleading in other ways, and cannot do the score justice. Lead sheets, were they included, can be sight-read by very few people.) Vitality—as a musical's most immediate market value—is best conveyed live.

At equal stake is that the writers are auditioning themselves. They have to seem capable in person of standing up to the pressures of seeing a musical through. They are also the material.

It should be no surprise if the total number of presentations fall between fifty and one hundred. It will take many presentations for different producers—Broadway, Off Broadway or New York institutional theaters (New York Shakespeare Festival, Chelsea Theatre Center, etc.)—before one will take an option. After the option is picked up, the producer also needs the writers to make presentations—to get investors (the so-called *backers' auditions*), to get a theater from theater owners, and audiences from theater party agents. To get enough investors, one theater, and some theater parties will take many more presentations. A musical may in addition go through several options for production, by different producers or renewals by the same producer. In *But He Doesn't Know the Territory*, Meredith Willson's saga of the production of **The Music Man,** Willson reports all the particulars that added up to seven years until opening night on Broadway. **Raisin,** according to one of its collaborators, took eight years; but according to another, nine. These are not slow times for a first Broadway musical.

It is not a presentation to do the entire musical. Not only is that likely to be baffling or strained, but, what is worse, the writers are making the occasion an abortive tryout. The purpose is only to bait the hook, initiate a business. Improving the presentation each time, by the way, frequently leads to improving the original.

A number of guideposts may be set forth. First, the presentation should run *under an hour.* Anything longer dissipates the impact. Second, it must suit the *informal* atmosphere of someone's office or, more likely, living room, for people looking for a *business investment.* Third, all of it must be performed by *less than a handful* of performers, and preferably only the writers, playing the fewest roles necessary.

As for the writers performing: having come this far, what else can be frightening? It is in fact on-the-job training for delivering under pressure. On the musical's behalf, moreover, no enlisted performer, however skillful, personable or partisan, can bring the originality or ardor to the material that its writers can. The very keying-up that all performing demands, stirred by their unique investment, may lead writers to out-do and surprise themselves. In any case, the anxiety of performing a presentation is far less than the anxiety of watching it.

If the writers believe their performing ability inferior to a professional's, *practicing* the presentation will improve it enough. (They even get bitten.) It should not, in fact, be brilliant piano-playing or singing. There have been presentations where the performance won more approval than the writing. Fred Ebb, lyricist of the Kander and Ebb team, is so vibrant a performer in auditions that one sometimes wonders if the writing is as good as he is. Jerry Herman, Sondheim and Lerner are ingratiating audition performers in other ways. But there have also been presentations where tinkly piano-playing or a sandy voice made enough impression because the writers performed with such connection. No one else is fit to convey the spirit of the material as faithfully, and whet the listeners' imagination as infectiously.

Only if performing abilities are nil—which is doubtful, having chosen this business—should writers involve others. A more accomplished pianist or one or two big voices, if a number or two demands them, may be included. But the simpler the selection and performance of songs is kept, the better. If others must carry a heavier musical load, then the writers should still insert themselves to do the simpler songs. Where the presentation requires brief narration, or merely some announcing of numbers, non-singing writers may appear. There have been presentations where the fervor or nimbleness of the narrator has helped decisively. The presentation needs most of all to be a show.

There are two chief ways to organize one. The obvious way is to follow the plot. As suggested earlier, a score that works is already a plot synopsis, which provides a head start in figuring out a presentation. There are pitfalls, however: the plot can be pursued too meticulously, or its description become complicated. The plot is bound to have flaws at this stage, suspected or not. And a plot never sold a musical. The idea and above all its songs sell it. If interest results, the script will be read as a consequence, a far easier way to convey the plot. Touching on it *loosely*, around the songs believed to be the most *entertaining*, is the way.

Eight songs or so, depending, usually add up to the limit of under an hour, with leeway for a reprise or two, an indication (only!) of a production number or two (someone always asks, "What are the production numbers?"), and encores on request (or not). Plugging what are hoped for as hits is often irresistible, but it is only a game. Every songwriter has a roll of the hits that missed, and of those that surprised.

The inclusion of samples of dialogue is to be avoided. An exception should be only to make an extraordinarily special point, and then kept to the barest minimum. The *business only* audience that is present is unique. It can be lost on the slightest pretext, and be even harder to retrieve. In the event that one song does not work, the next is the easiest way to recover. Even in introducing each song, or if possible groupings of songs, shun the traps of words. Fire the best shots, music. The master criterion is not what makes the musical work but what makes the presentation work.

An alternate way favored by some is less obvious, but sometimes less cumbersome than following the plot. Songs are selected mainly for their showmanship, such as their ingenuity or reach, or their variety and contrast. A sequence of its own is then shaped, in which style becomes the accent. This offers an incidental advantage—practice in *routining*, a warm-up for rehearsals and tryout to come. Plot values cannot be completely eliminated in such routining, for that would ignore the very basis of show songwriting. But it teaches how to keep plot relative.

Which one to employ will vary with every musical, and other bases for presentations may suggest themselves—as long as a *show* every time is the goal. Whatever the way in working it out, it is not a disgrace but a help to "think dumb." Let nothing be taken for granted; test every assumption. Stay simple and clear. And peddle.

The Creative Staff

The presentation finally wins a producer. He proceeds to the musical's capitalization, and begins the assembly of a director, a choreographer, a musical director (the conductor) and set, costume and lighting designers. Musical arrangers will follow. The writers will rarely be alone again. These are the new collaborators, some more than others, for the rest of the way. They comprise the *creative staff*. They can be extraordinary allies.

Or not. In such cases, a solid front on the writers' part is more important than ever: private disagreements are better kept to themselves. Writers may say yes to many suggestions, but only if the head and the stomach assent together; otherwise they must learn to say no. That is not as easy as it seems. The talent around them, usually high-powered and often high-priced, will be thick and persuasive. Beware of being grateful for it; let it prove itself like everything else. The writers supply the new and fresh talent, which everyone else then gets aboard. No one can know more about the generating idea. The creative staff should only know more about how to make it work. It is better to forgo an option, or even close a show in tryout, than do a different show from the one the writers intended; but only the first flop will teach that.

Veto power is written into the Dramatists Guild Contract, the standard agreement writers sign for a Broadway or Off Broadway musical production. Writers may not be able to insist on every one of their ideas (they can be wrong, too), but they can turn down any ideas that others may offer. This applies not only to rewrite suggestions, but also to any piece of casting, from creative staff to performers, and any production ideas, from designs to orchestrations. More, not a single word or note written may be changed anywhere, without the writers' express permission.

Of course, producers, directors, choreographers, designers, arrangers—and stars—have all developed gambits to get around this veto power. These include threats to abandon the production, appeals to help keep the budget down, advice during casting that certain actors are better to work with than others, or warnings that some approaches or details will be too difficult, too technical or too unsuitable. The ingenuity is sometimes fascinating to behold.

The trap for writers is being drawn into someone else's problems. The remedy is to measure every objection on its own merits. Struggles will occur among the best of people and the best of staffs, and honest struggles produce better shows. In the last analysis, collaboration is chemistry, but the catalyst is humor. The mischief of egotism is that it stops ideas from coming first.

If there were a Table of Organization for a musical, it would look like this:

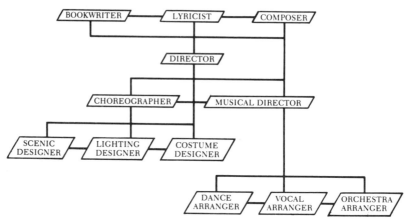

Some of these combine. The musical director may also be one of the arrangers, perhaps the vocal arranger. All the arrangers are assistants of the musical director; more specifically, they make up the staff of the composer and musical director, rather than belonging as general members to the creative staff. The vocal arranger may of course be a separate specialist, or the orchestra arranger as well. The vocal arranger's jobs include conducting the ensemble vocal rehearsals and sometimes the principal vocal rehearsals (under the composer's and musical director's authority), and he may also be the vocal rehearsal pianist. The dance arranger is likely to be the dance rehearsal pianist. Similarly, the scenic designer may also be the lighting or costume designer. Most important, the director may also be the choreographer.

The director is the hub. A chief part of his function is, so to speak, as midwife to everyone else's imagination—the writers', the choreographer's, the musical director's, the designers', and the actors'. His own directional inspiration is fundamental, however—creating, executing or supervising all the production ideas. Yet equally crucial is his ability to be overall artistic administrator. Rehearsals and tryout are extremely complex and departmentalized processes. Unless the *daily* work is centralized and distributed by him, chaos reigns. The director is the only creative staff member with direct access to everyone. If he is good at administration, he will know how to delegate assignments, with whom to deal, when—and when not.

For instance, he must know music, but he is better off not trying to be a musical specialist; he has a whole department for that, under the composer and the musical director, the composer's right hand. If he has any suggestions or questions about the music's sound, he goes to them, not to the arrangers. He himself, in other words, sets the example of respecting channels.

Specifically, his duty is directing the *book rehearsals*, that is, all the dialogue scenes. He is responsible in *every* area for the acting competence—be it verbal, vocal or physical.

The composer is in a special situation. He is in command of every musical sound that comes off the stage or from the pit, written directly by him or delegated. The composer is the only one of the writers, accordingly, who may by-pass the director to work directly with the musical director and the arrangers. But he must be careful to keep the director informed of everything which affects the performance on stage, as the only way to ensure follow-through of his wishes.

But! No one but the director, the musical director (and his arranger-assistants) and the choreographer may deal directly with the actors! Even when the songwriters participate in the learning and rehearsal of songs, it may be only in conjunction with designated members of the staff under the director, or with the director himself. Confusion takes over irreparably if writers intercede personally, on their own, with any single performer, or set of performers. Performers can cope only with the directions organized from one source. *All* questions or suggestions that the writers may have about what happens on stage, including choreography and scenery, go to the director *only*. He alone takes the appropriate action.

The choreographer needs certain leeways of access, under the director's warrant. The choreographer has already been described as a valuable co-author, so he obviously needs to work with all the writers. This will include, in conjunction with the director, the final *routining* of the show. In rehearsal and tryout, for instance, "brick-re-laying" processes are constant. What song finally follows what song, what scene or part of a scene is shuffled, and what may be consequently required, including new songs and scenes, to put the show back together—these are the things sometimes not "frozen" until just before the New York opening.

The choreographer likewise needs access to the designers. His deployment of people in space makes him also a co-designer. This starts with the scenic designs, in which there must be room to move, onstage and off; moreover, the mobile patterns are often what complete the spatial designs. It also starts with the costume designs, which must be workable not only to dance in, but also to change in and out of *quickly*. Obviously it includes the lighting design, to pinpoint and highlight the movement and costumes, sometimes the most exacting operation of all. The choreographer must also be an expert in administration.

All along, the choreographer needs access to the musical director. The choreographer is not a co-composer. And yet in one way he is, for which he has a "private interpreter," the dance arranger. Show dance music cannot be properly composed in advance. The choreographer needs to adapt or invent rhythmic and sometimes thematic musical figures in varying phrase lengths (all in counts!) from the score, directly out of his rehearsals with the dancers. If the dance arranger is not the rehearsal pianist, he is present making notes nonetheless. The result will be the dance music, literally or in spirit out of the score. Dance arrangement, it goes without saying, is a supremely skilled and specialized profession. Subject as always to the composer, this music must then be relayed to the musical director—he will have to conduct it. Some conductors are better with singers, others with dancers. The amount of coordination required among choreographer, dance arranger and musical director, to get and *keep* the tempos, the dynamics and many other details, takes the utmost pains and practice. It is almost unheard of for everyone ever to feel completely satisfied. But the number gets on.

There are three items that writers ought to know about direction and choreography. After the obvious distinction between staging straight dance numbers and straight dialogue scenes, the division of labor between choreographer and director is mixed. "Musical staging" by the choreographer usually means that every segment of moving to music is staged by him. "Dances and musical numbers" by the choreographer usually means the same thing. "Choreography" by the choreographer usually means that all dances have been staged by him but not all songs.

Out of my own experience as a director, I have come to prefer the last arrangement. The director is generally consulted about the choice of choreographer. As director, he has final artistic responsibility for every part of the show, and the choreographer must be subject, like everyone else on the creative staff, to the director's authority. I find results more satisfying when I stage most ballads and comedy numbers, which require no dance *steps*. It is obvious that in practice this division becomes one of the stickiest relationships in the production process, yet together director and choreographer must share a great deal of work. Ideally, an audience should not be able to tell where one leaves off and the other begins.

Item two is that one of the effects of this latent conflict has been the rise of the choreographer as overall director. In that capacity, he may have a "book director" working under him; if he himself directs the dialogue scenes, he may then have an assistant choreographer. There is too much work for one person alone. Why choreographers have successfully taken over direction—Jerome Robbins, Bob Fosse, Gower Champion, Michael Bennett and others—is an intriguing speculation. They have an acute sense of how physically alive a musical ought to look, and the means in their own hands (and feet) of accomplishing it. They also have a built-in and highly trained appreciation of the storytelling power of movement, and often of the showmanship of musical theater. Many directors have such a "psychological" bent that they encourage results too static and introspective for the outgoing, high-key kinetics of musical theater. On the other hand, the acting in a choreographer-directed musical may fall short, because only a few choreographers feel at home here.

Thirdly, one of the most glaring but least likely reforms due in musical theater is to involve both director and choreographer far earlier in the writing phase. In practice, it occurs only a little before casting and rehearsals—but always too late. The obstacles are two, and formidable. No budget exists to pay them earlier when they need to be engaged, while writers who enlist their help earlier have no power to guarantee that the eventual producer will engage them. When director and choreographer are finally hired, their situation is always one of catching up—a deplorable condition.

The final area of collaboration between writers and creative staff is design. The writers participate in the director's and choreographer's groundwork with the designers. Not that the writers must bring any design expertise—they are present less to be specific than to corroborate that their vision of the musical is caught and enhanced.

The producer has been omitted because it is a question whether he is a member of the creative staff. From a business standpoint, of course, he is at the top, one of the last survivors of "rugged individualism," the entrepreneur manager. He finds the property, raises the money, organizes the operation, controls costs, and if successful, maintains and distributes the product.

Within the creative area, however, there are two kinds of producers: those who delegate, and those who participate. When entertaining the musical for optioning, both kinds may make creative demands of the writers. The first do so as a condition of their purchase, but leave the writers alone on the presumption that it is their job to figure out the answers. The second do so by working personally with the writers; the chance to participate may be one of the deepest motivations they have for being producers. But the second need to be first-rate at it. Throughout auditions, rehearsals and tryout, they must take as much care as the director not to bypass or break through the staff channels, or they destroy their own production.

The creative staff should be allowed to create, united into a staff.

Rehearsal and Tryout

Books published on the productions of particular musicals are all logs of stormy voyages. Rehearsal and tryout are two of the stormiest passages.

The start of rehearsals means the musical gets on its feet. The difference is acute, at first either exhilarating or devastating. The show is being transformed from the dreamed-up, untested page to the physical, demanding stage. Every word and note becomes subject to live performers. The idea works or not through people.

Everyone pours energy into the biggest effort of all now—to bring script, music and performers to excellence. Performers in turn inspire writers and staff to excel. The "Marian Mercer bit" is a not infrequent occurrence: a performer comes through so well in rehearsal and tryout, as Ms. Mercer did in **Promises, Promises**, that the role is expanded. The *bit* could be named for others. On the other hand, the jolt of casting changes is more likely. However painful on all sides, the need to make the show right, as well as one is able to judge, takes entire precedence.

The sooner something clearly wrong is fixed, in casting, direction or writing, the better. Sometimes remedies can be taken too soon, however: trial and error should be given a full run. Some things take more nurturing, or ripen on their own. Every revision has a ripple effect, moreover, requiring other alterations down the line. Above all, every song added or removed reshapes the show. In sum, the process of finding out more and more exactly what is needed is unremitting. But it means the work is going right.

Inevitable will be blocks and log-jams. There are no formulas to break them. Keeping intuition open, staying particular, and stamina are some basic resorts. Perception, not conception, is above all talent's strength. A member of my workshop had two ideas for a musical: a generation-gap story, and a college story. Each got stymied, but in both an older married couple kept appearing. That couple was what was in the writer's depths, his real subject; yet he could not see it. The obvious is often elusive.

The rehearsal method of musicals starts as bits and pieces. Actors Equity Association regulations set the Broadway musical rehearsal period at five weeks: the dancers alone for the first week, principals and all the rest of the cast for the remaining four weeks. Rehearsal space requires several working areas: dancers in one location, singers in another, principals in a third, various groupings gradually mixing and shaping together, in different combinations ranging throughout the script. The logistics of these shifting arrangements every day, all day long, are a large part of the director's administrative pains. Progressively, however, more and more is combined until it culminates in what is called the *put together,* the first complete *run-through.*

An exciting moment. The process of trial and error takes a leap forward as the whole begins to be seen. This immediately reveals the lapses that need to be fixed—proportions, holes, blurs, derailments, and on and on. The rehearsal time is now split between *bits and pieces* sessions and the *put togethers.*

Then come the next biggest moments. The tryout period begins, testing the show with audiences; they become its director, the most responsive there is. The last thing a show needs is to be "catered" or "programmed" to the audience—though many actual directors try—counting laughs and calculating tears. But an audience is more versatile than the finest artist. It will go as it is treated, responding cheaply or conventionally if so addressed, with extraordinary imagination if so led. A show needs to suggest.

Robert Russell Bennett, dean of musical arrangers, was once asked, "Are there any forces or movements leading to the improvement of musicals?" With more than fifty musicals behind him, including many of the great hits from **Show Boat** to **My Fair Lady**, he answered in about these words: "I don't believe in such things. That's not the work of writers. Everyone who writes a musical is simply trying to do something fresher, newer, never touched before, and better than anyone else, including his own last work."

The *seed* and the vision of the musical minister most acutely to this. In the strains which mount incessantly right up to the New York opening, these are exactly what get torn away or crunched. Lose them, lose all. To reiterate: the most valuable member of all the collaborators is he who can keep the original inspiration clear and steady.

The Money, and Other Rewards

The business side of the theater is another subject, with books to itself. What will have to suffice here is the barest outline of one of its most intricate aspects, the writers' share of the money.

Theater writers are paid not on a fee basis but by royalties in percentages. The "Dramatists Guild, Inc. Minimum Basic Production Contract" provides for a combined authors' minimum percentage of a weekly 6% of the *gross* receipts, from the day of the first paid audience, whether New York preview or tryout out of town. (After a hit, the minimums will be bettered in future contracts.) If there are three collaborators, they share equally in thirds; if two, equally in half; if more than three, the shares are divided equally again. This percentage is *off the top;* that is, before any operating expenses are deducted. If a musical is in a theater, for instance, whose seating is scaled at prices to gross, in round figures, $100,000 weekly at capacity (every seat sold), each member of a three-collaborator team receives $2,000 a week. If the musical is touring in more than one theater outside of New York, multiply by the number of theaters. This includes the United Kingdom, where the royalty agreements are the same. If running elsewhere abroad, the royalties vary by country, and are negotiated.

The *option* is an advance against royalties. Against the total royalties possible from a success, it is microscopic—yet its minuteness is the appropriate gamble for both writers and producer, in order to start. The option is for the exclusive right to produce the musical within a specified period of time. There may be variations, but generally it amounts to $500 for the first three months, $100 each month for the next three months, and $200 each month for the next six months. Sometimes this is condensed to a payment of $2,000-2,500 for a year's option (the common period), with say, $1,000 down, and the remainder to be paid on an agreed schedule over the year. Options are renewable beyond a year, all parties agreeing to carry-over terms. These payments are divided among the writers again in equal portions.

After the Broadway run and national tours, all classified as *first class*—a legal, not an artistic term—there are then *second class* tour possibilities. These refer to "bus and truck" tours, one-nighters, night club circuits and college circuits. *Subsidiary* royalties follow. These are the royalties from stock theaters, dinner theaters, university and high school theaters, and community (amateur) theaters. This category adds up to thousands of theaters, some of which may play the musical more than once, paying varying rates of royalties or of set fees. Over the years the writers will earn more from these *subsidiary rights* than from the original, complete *first class* run!

It does not stop here. There are the movie sale rights. The authors receive 60% of the sale price, the producer 40%. Again this is equally divided among the writers, with added percentages, if included, of box office receipts from the film. If the rights are sold, say, for a million dollars (a low figure today), each writer gets $200,000 to begin, box office royalties to come. There are complexities here that require contract specialists.

Add original cast album rights from the stage production, and sound track recording rights from the film production. Add royalties on single record sales, sheet music sales, and television and radio performances of the songs. By this time, a music publisher is playing a large role, to promote the score—and share in the royalties. The percentages from this area of income on a successful show are variously negotiable, but astronomical. Long before this time, an agent, a lawyer, an accountant, or a personal manager—or all of them—will have had to represent the writers in handling these arrangements.

On some of them, involving songs alone, the bookwriter shares to a lesser extent. He has play publication prospects, however, which the composer has not. The lyricist participates equally both ways. *Middle-income theater* royalties, Off Broadway royalties, and institutional and regional theater royalties all follow the same patterns, with less total income but no grounds for complaint.

So preposterous odds were licked, with preposterous rewards. The musical may have proceeded in new directions, too, in new kinds of song, dance or dialogue, or new balances of them. In manner, it may have been more playful and irreverent than ever before, or in character study, sharper and deeper, or in form, further into *collage*; it may have invented ways, indeed, that will need new names to describe them.

The old American musical is past: never-say-die optimism, ending in love happily ever after. The new American musical is still building: broken rhythm, up-tempo drives fertile and reaching, impelled by the energy of the most dance-crazed and dance-adept nation in history. Yet the original Greek stage *orchestra* was a "dancing place," and *theatron* a "seeing place." Stories told through popular song and dance are taking over as a new theater of cathartic power and life force. The best musicals make audible the music under so many moments of living, and make visible the dance behind so many gestures. Some may even be, in Thurber's phrase, fables for our time, but all are celebrations of the tryouts of life made triumphs.

Index

177